A Day

In the

Life of Death

A Behind the Scenes

Look at the

Mortuary Business

by

Ryan M. Lee

Foreword

Over the last generation the "funeral business" has transformed itself into the "death care industry". In the last ten years the industry has seen the rise and fall of huge corporate providers, the creation of wildly popular televisions programs based on the "reality" of the funeral home life as well as horrible scandals in the Bay Area of California and the rural South that have people wondering if they can trust their crematory operator to properly cremate, let alone scatter their loved ones cremated remains as requested.

How can anyone filter through the hype of television sensationalism, sterile financial journals or newspaper headlines to discover what really happens in the funeral home? The truth is that it is impossible to know the things that go unseen. No matter how respectable the journalist, how detailed the accountant or how creative the screen writer, a person who hasn't lived the life of death cannot completely articulate the real life drama of an industry shrouded in secrecy.

Consider this book your inside guide, your map to the stars or your friend in the business. You will come to learn what goes on, where it happens and even how to save money when making funeral arrangements. So please, sit back, relax and enjoy this tour of an industry that often runs from the limelight.

This book is dedicated to my wife, who has had to live with and helped me as I worked through many of the issues caused by my years in the funeral business.

I further dedicate this book to my son, who has motivated me and taught me so very much.

Table of Contents:

Chapter One

Here am I

It may come as a shock to you that I actually had a life before I was a mortician. I have come across scores of people who, when talking with them about my career as an embalmer, say "You know, that's a job that I never thought about anyone actually doing". I wasn't born a mortician and contrary to what most people assume, no one else in my family had worked in the funeral industry prior to me.

I was actually born the youngest of ten children, an even split between boys and girls. I was raised attending church every week and attended public schools. My father was an Assistant Program Director for a State Hospital and my mother was a nurse for the local district hospital.

I grew up with the "normal" hopes and dreams of every red blooded American boy. In the fifth grade I had decided to become a "Rock Star". After all, if Buddy Holly could do it, so could I. By eighth grade my music career had fallen flat and I turned my attention to my pro-athlete career. Bo Jackson made it look so easy! Why couldn't I play football and baseball professionally? The main reason I wouldn't grow up to wear both a World Series and Super Bowl ring is because I lack those talents needed to do so.

As I entered high school I floundered a bit and became involved in everything from the YMCA, "Youth in Government" program to the FFA. I even had a somewhat successful career as a high school tuba player and enjoyed most of the other things that teenagers did.

Growing up, and even now, my musical taste included artists like Waylon Jennings, The Statler Brothers, The Grateful Dead, The Beatles, Simon and Garfunkel and Cake, the band not the treat. I just love "good" music. I was especially partial to singer/songwriters like Jim Croce, Bob Dylan, Buddy Holly and the Mama's and the Papa's. Not to leave out the truly wonderful sounds of "Motown" and Jazz.

Due to the fact that my parents had sent me to kindergarten at the age of four, I graduated from high school at the age of seventeen. My funeral service career started the summer following my graduation from high school.

I started working for a local; family owned and operated funeral home in the Central Valley of California. By the time I was eighteen I had buried my fifth grade teacher, an Olympic Gold Medallist and cleared more suicide scenes than I care to remember.

Shortly after I was hired it became expected of me, by my employer, that I would enroll in the "Premier" Mortuary College to complete my Funeral Service studies. I was accepted into and completed my Associates Degree at the San Francisco College of Mortuary Science, commonly referred to as "the Princeton of Mortuary Colleges".

At the completion of my mortuary science education I moved from the San Francisco Bay Area to the Willamette Valley of Oregon. There I worked for, at the time, the largest funeral service provider company in the world, Service Corporation International (SCI). Service Corp. owned a large cluster of funeral homes between Portland and Roseburg, Oregon. Even though I had completed my formal education and had a couple of years experience under my belt, I learned a great deal about marketing, merchandising and branding while in the employ of this company. I learned many things that I would incorporate into my routine and some things that I would avoid like the plague from then on. I left SCI shortly after they merged with Equity Corp. International. ECI was a company that was created by a group of funeral homes and cemeteries that had been "spun off" by SCI in order to obtain approval by the Federal Government to purchase a larger number of businesses in more "strategic" markets.

Seeking a simpler workday that would require fewer reports and more consistency, I went to work for another "family owned and operated" firm in Eastern Oregon. It was there that I discovered that some jobs aren't worth having. I worked for a husband and wife who were in the process of buying the funeral home from the lady's father. The father had spent years building the business and he spent decades in the service of his community. However, I believe the daughter will in short order run the family business into the ground. Her husband is a nice enough, decent man, but she is insecure, untrusting and a severe micro-manager. After several months of torturous mental strain, I left Eastern Oregon and I took a job in Southern California to work for, at that time the second largest Funeral Service provider in the nation, Lowen Group International.

It has been said by those in the business that, "SCI is businessmen acting like funeral directors and Lowen Group is Funeral Directors acting like businessmen". Having worked for both companies I hold a similar opinion. Within months of being hired by Lowen, they filed for bankruptcy and announced that they were selling the cluster of funeral homes that were in my geographical area.

After years of broken promises from management, and being sold off, I left the "corporate" world behind. I must admit that it was working for Lowen that burned me out professionally; the never-ending drama of pending sales, audits and internal office politics. I left Lowen and even wondered if I should leave the business altogether. It was the miserable work environment at Lowen that acted as my greatest motivator. In frustration, I went back to college. I had enrolled in Chapman University, located in Orange California, and had begun my journey out of the funeral service industry.

Unaware that I was mentally and emotionally burned-out and in need of a few more semesters to complete my Bachelors Degree, I went to work for the best place that I have ever worked. I took a position as an embalmer for a company owned by an elderly husband and wife team. When I started working there it was easy for me to overlook the fact that I was burned out, due in large part to the people that I worked for and with. The entire staff were wonderful people to be around. I enjoyed nearly every moment that I had with them. Sadly, shortly after I started my new job the owner was forced to retire due to health issues that would eventually take his life.

This type of unexpected change can often lead to family battles and staff walkouts, however, none of that happened here. The staff consisted of two other embalmers, both of whom had worked for this company for over twenty-five years, the bookkeeper who was a very delightful and compassionate woman, and the office manager, who was an optimistic and cheery lady, who also happened to be the daughter-in-law of the owners. It was my love of these people and the joy of working with them that kept me in the funeral business for a few more years.

What you have learned of me thus far could not answer the question of why I became a mortician? The framework has only been laid, the answer lies within the details. How old were you when you saw your first dead body? Who was it? I was seven years old and it was my Grandfather. He died from complications of Diabetes. My mom suffered the heartache of loosing both her mom and her dad within four months of each other. My

Grandmother died of lung cancer just months after my grandfather had died.

That year my mother was terribly saddened and she was not intentionally distant, but her sadness took her to places that it became difficult for her to navigate a "normal" life from. My mom was very close to her mother and called her almost daily to chat and it was only the distance of death that broke this habit of regular communications. As a matter of fact, it was on one of these routine calls to each other that my grandmother died. Imagine hearing your mom's last breath from one thousand miles away.

My father has always been a constant and supportive man. I always count myself lucky to have been his son. He was forty-seven at the time of my birth and I never had a chance to meet either of his parents. His mother died when he was a young child and his father died the year prior to my birth. I firmly believe that this lack of grandparents from such a young age plays a great deal into whom I have become friends with.

During my childhood, my mom worked nights at the local hospital and would arrive at home from work typically after my dad had woke us up, made us breakfast and gotten us ready for school.

During the time after my mom's parent's died he tried to lighten mom's load around the house by taking us kids to places to stay out of my mom's hair. We would take drives up to the lake, walk around the swap meet or any other free activity that could keep a heard of children occupied.

Unfortunately after less than a year tragedy would strike our family. My oldest brother Steve, who had recently returned from a church mission, was killed in an industrial accident while at work. That was the first time I had ever seen my Dad cry.

The accident happened in early August, and my oldest sister Debbie had just taken me, along with her children, to the Fresno Zoo. When we returned home, it was obvious that something bad had happened.

As for my brother's funeral, I remember as we were walking into the church behind Steve's casket, one of my nephews asked, "Why is Uncle Steve in that old, dusty box?" Everywhere I looked I saw heartache and pain. I saw brothers and sisters devastated and parents so consumed by their own pains that they could hardly keep themselves together. How could they offer comfort to others in their state of misery? I can still recall the look of broken dreams on the face of Steve's fiancé, as she sat there in the "family" section. I truly regret to say that I haven't seen her since the funeral.

Months later, I sat in my classroom on a cold, foggy January morning only to helplessly watch replay after replay, the death of the seven Space Shuttle Challenger Astronauts. I still remember to this day how comforting President Ronald Reagan's address to the Nation was for me. The Challenger disaster reminded me of my first exposure to TV violence, and that was when at the age of three years old, I watched the man who was now comforting me through the television set, being shot by a would be assassin as he left a Washington D.C. Hotel. Television and primarily CNN brought death to me daily in thirty-minute intervals. However, that night President Reagan's words spoke of hope, honor and a greater good. There was no mention of despair or hopelessness. President Reagan helped me accept death when he said:

"The crew of the space shuttle Challenger honored us by the manner in which they lived their lives. We will never forget them, nor the last time we saw them, this morning, as they prepared for their journey and waved goodbye and 'slipped the surly bonds of earth' to touch the face of God."

As time went by and the pain of the three very real losses of family members could still be felt, I recall my dad saying that it took three years to finally feel "normal" after Steve had died. He didn't say to "get over it", just to feel "normal".

I had finally made it to the sixth grade and my life was progressing "normally". Then on Easter Sunday, the Principal of my elementary school was killed when a train, at an unmarked and low visibility railroad crossing, struck the car he was driving. He was killed not far from his home.

His loss was great to me, but not as traumatic on the entire family as the deaths of close family members. When I went to his visitation at the funeral home, I spent more time looking at him, almost studying him. I closely examined the makeup that was obviously placed in an attempt to cover his injuries from the accident. However, my youth and immature understanding of life and death was evident, due to the fact that at his viewing I can recall the fear that he might come back from the dead, showing that I did not have a true appreciation of the finality of death.

Once again CNN would import violence and murder into my mind via the television. In 1988, USMC LTC William Higgins, was kidnapped, tortured and murdered by pro-Iranian terrorist in Lebanon. I, to this day, remember the swing motion of Col. Higgins lifeless body as he hung from the rafters of a prison cell.

Between the ages of eleven to fifteen my life was void of death. My Dad had a couple of heart attacks; one bout with bladder cancer and my Mom had a radical hysterectomy. However, nobody died. That was about to change.

My freshman year in high school I learned that one of my dearest friends from elementary school, a kid who lived almost across the street from me, and a person that routinely spent the night at my house, would soon die from cancer. He was just a kid, my age, who loved sports, and who was a kind person. He did not deserve the fate he was handed.

He had a mole removed by his doctor. They told him that they would call him if the mole was malignant. They never called him, and he died because of it. After his first bout with Chemo Therapy the doctors said there was no hope for him. They offered him a second round of Chemo to "lengthen" his life. He refused the second round. The Chemo Therapy made him sick. He preferred to live fewer days with better quality.

High Schools are small communities; each death creates waves and ripples, if for no other reason than you are reminded of your own mortality. For every year I was in high school someone from our campus died. Some died in car accidents, a couple to meningitis, and three to suicide. These deaths served as a reminder to me that none of us are getting out of this life alive.

Through all of this and up to this point in my life, I was determined to go into law or more likely politics. I loved the "game" of politics. My political hero Lee Atwater was a "No Holds Barred" political consultant. Karl Rove couldn't shine his shoes. While other kids thought of playing basketball with Larry Bird or Magic Johnson, I wanted to run a campaign with Lee. Known as the "Darth Vader" of the Republican Party, his scorched earth tactics created wins. I never had a chance to work with Karl Rove's mentor, the "Great" Lee Atwater; he died of a brain tumor. However, he and his death taught me much about the importance of life.

In a February 1991 article for *Life Magazine*, Atwater wrote:

"My illness helped me to see that what was missing in society is what was missing in me: a little heart, a lot of brotherhood. The 80's were about acquiring -- acquiring wealth, power, and prestige. I know. I acquired more wealth, power, and prestige that most. But you can acquire all you want and still feel empty. What power wouldn't I trade for a little more time with my family? What price wouldn't I pay for an evening with friends? It took a deadly illness to put me eye to eye with that truth, but it is a truth that the country, caught up in its ruthless ambitions and moral decay, can learn on my dime. I don't know who will lead us through the 90's, but they must be made to speak to this spiritual vacuum at the heart of American society, this tumor of the soul."

Surely the simple fact that I knew people who had died did not drive me to be a mortician; however, I do feel that it created a predisposition in me to understand the humanity behind death combined with a learned ability to compartmentalize my emotions. All that was missing was a motive.

That motive came on the Thanksgiving of my senior year in high school. Most families have that "fun" or "crazy" uncle, my mother's brother was mine, and on that day he died from complications following hip replacement surgery. His wife, my aunt, trusted her local funeral and cemetery (combination) provider to help her through this sudden death. All that they did for her was empty her pocket book as much as they could. This was not enough to create in me a desire to serve in or change the funeral business, but the fact that the funeral director wore a Los Angeles Rams lapel pin to his funeral service was. How dare this "clown" wear such an infuriating pin? Most of my family is comprised of die-hard San Francisco Forty-Niner fans and my uncle loved the Seattle Seahawks. Such a disrespectful action would have me declaring a personal war on the funeral industry. All I needed was a job in a funeral home. How do you get one of those?

Chapter Two

Should I be a

mortician?

So, you want to be a mortician? Do you have what it takes? How do you get your "big break"? Many times during my career people have asked me how they too could be either an embalmer or a funeral director. Several of the people who have asked me that question have given me a feeling of great apprehension or pause for thought at the mere idea of having to call that individual a "colleague".

If you or someone you know is considering the funeral service industry as a possible career path, I would encourage that person to seriously look within themselves and ask a few not so obvious questions.

Can I physically handle the work?

Imagine routinely being woken up in the middle of the night from a sound sleep to go to work. People die at all hours of the day and night.

It used to be said that, "No one died before 6a.m.". However, just like every other facet of our lives, death doesn't take a break. No longer do people discover the death of a loved one when they awake in the morning. Nursing homes, hospice, and hospitals all contribute to the sleepless night of the mortician. If you are a person who cannot function on limited sleep, you may want to revisit your choice of funeral service as a career path.

You have most likely seen the reports on the news, as well as the people walking around your town, Americans are getting fatter. Just one season of "The Biggest Loser" or "Jamie Oliver's Food Revolution" will give you a great view into how we're bulking up as a society. If you want to be a mortician, ask yourself: Are you able to physically move someone your size or larger? Sure, there might be someone there to help if the death occurred in a hospital or car accident, but who will help you when you get back to the mortuary in the middle of the night? If you are reading this and thinking of needing others to help you do your job, I suggest that you reconsider your career path. Please ask yourself, "Would I want me to help myself?" If the answer is no, then odds are that the people you will be working with won't want your help either.

It would be convenient for the mortician if everyone died in a bed, in a room with easy access for a gurney. However, you will encounter spiral staircases, forty-five degree angles and countless other unmovable objects that will make removing a decedent from their place of death a very challenging task. Some of the more challenging "removals" that I have been part of included a person who died in their bathtub, another who died in the small bathroom of a mobile home, several people who had hanged themselves from various objects with varying distances from the ground. However the most difficult decedents to remove have been the "morbidly obese". I have had to remove doors and walls, employ hydraulic lifts and other devices of manipulation in an effort to do my job. A great deal of physical strength and an even larger amount of mental creativity is often employed to move those people who weigh four hundred pounds or more.

Can I physically handle what I will see, smell, touch and hear?

I will confess to you now that the only thing that makes me retch is the smell of fecal matter. What makes you sick? Is it the sight of blood, the smell of vomit, the touch of a urine soaked garment of clothing? These are the everyday occurrences in the life of the mortician. Much worse things happen on the bad days. Seeing the calamity of a multi-fatality accident, smelling the unforgettable odors associated with cancer, bed sores; gangrenous wounds and decomposition of human remains all etch indelible memories on ones sensory system.

Will you be able to continue with your workday, let alone your family life, after seeing the affects of a multi-car pile-up, or the scene of a family murdered in cold-blood? Will you be able to go home to your spouse and children and give to them all that they need, or will you continuously look to others to pull you through the "rough" day that you had?

Can I emotionally handle the job?

Some of the hardest days at work that I have had were due to the "personal stories" that I had learned about the decedent and their families. One that comes to my mind daily is the story of a four-year-old girl. This little girl was the only child of an unmarried mother who, in my opinion, was not a very good mother. The mother, the little girl, and the mother's "date" had checked into the local "No Tell Motel". The mother and her date proceeded to engage in various sex acts while the daughter was in the room; the daughter quickly became bored and wanted to watch the TV. Due to the fact that the adults in the room were preoccupied with their own "needs", the daughter went to turn the TV on. The little girl started to climb up the dresser and as she reached for the power button, the weight balance of the dresser became unstable and it shifted. The dresser and the TV set tipped over crushing the child.

Many heart breaking stories like this will happen over the years for the person serving and working in the funeral business. When stories like this are told, or unfold before your eyes, you must be able to deal with the family with the professionalism that is offered to every other family. In the previous story I aided the family with their funeral service planning. The mother's only concern was, "How much will it cost me?" The funeral home donated its services, and the motel owner, out of their own sympathy bought the headstone for the child. I know that the family paid us no money for the funeral or the cemetery costs, however, "How much will it cost" her? I have no idea.

After an emotionally draining day, you will have to have the ability to go home, open the mail, have dinner with your family and put the kids to bed. If you do not think that you'll be able to do that, perhaps you should consider another vocation.

Will my family tolerate my work schedule?

How many times will your spouse let you miss an anniversary because you are on-call? How many Christmas mornings are you willing to leave your home to "clear" a drunken driver accident scene? How many late night romantic interludes between you and your lover are you willing to give up, so that you can go to work? If you do not want to be a 24/7 employee, then the mortuary business is not for you. I, and all of my co-workers and colleagues, have had to "prioritize" which nights we wanted off and we have all had to give up "special occasions" for work. Do you work your birthday so that you can have your son's off? Do you work Thanksgiving so that you can have Christmas off? Do you give up Valentine's Day in a trade for your anniversary or your spouse's birthday? Special occasions taken for granite by the nine to five professionals become bargaining chips on the funeral home work schedule. Will you trade Mother's Day for Father's Day?

Am I clean enough to keep my family safe?

I have been asked countless times "Are you afraid of AIDS?" My answer is always the same, "AIDS is the least of my worries!" I then go on to explain that the HIV/AIDS virus is a very weak virus and the life of the virus ends with cellular death of the body. That means that after death, if you wait approximately 24 hours prior to embalming a decedent who has the AIDS virus; the risk of contracting the virus is greatly diminished. However, there are scarier diseases to work with during the preparation of the dead.

Hepatitis is a disease that comes in three strains A, B and C. Varying strands can be contracted through multiple forms of contamination. Hepatitis C is by far the most dangerous and deadly form of the disease. Most health care professionals will tell you that to contract Hepatitis C one would have to have an intrusive incident leading to direct blood exposure such as a needle stick or blood transfusion. This would leave most people feeling that the only person being placed at risk is the embalmer, I caution you otherwise.

At times during the embalming process blood could easily and accidentally spill onto the floor. This would then make it very easy for the embalmer to either step into the blood or have the blood drip unnoticed onto his black wingtip shoes. After cleaning the blood from the floor and calling it a day this embalmer then goes home, where inevitably he will walk into his home and across his carpet. It is here that the entire family has a risk of exposure.

Your infant crawling across the carpet in an excited effort to see their parent unknowingly picks-up the virus on a moist finger that she has been sucking on and is then eagerly picked up into the arms of the returning parent. At this point the child is pleased, and she then remembers why she was sucking on her finger, she's teething. The child then inserts the contaminated finger back into her mouth and directly upon the bloody, open sore in her mouth where her new tooth is coming in.

This story can be repeated for nearly every child in the home, the toddler picking scabs or his nose, the adolescent who lies on the floor in front of the TV picking at the "road rash" injury from their skate boarding efforts earlier in the day. Everyone in the home is at risk of contracting blood borne pathogens, if the people working with them do not practice minimum procedures to ensure maximum precautions.

I have illustrated how easy it could be to expose your entire family to a very serious blood borne pathogen. Hepatitis C is the toughest form of Hepatitis to contract. Imagine on your own how much easier the exposure will come from Hepatitis A and B. There is actually one other disease that I would feel negligent if I did not mention. It is not contracted by needle stick and the process of embalming won't necessarily increase your exposure to it.

Tuberculosis is becoming more common in many parts of the United States, especially those with a large illegal immigrant population. Disease control efforts in California and the Southwest are failing due to the fact that a more aggressive and drug resistant form of the bacterial infection is spreading. Imagine a disease that all you have to do to contract it is breathe the air of someone who has it. You may be saying to yourself, well that isn't all that serious, since the people that the mortician works with aren't breathing. If you assume that attitude, you will be dead wrong!

As I have mentioned before, not all people die in easily accessible areas. Imagine one of the decedents that you have to move down a spiral staircase or around a 45-degree turn has Tuberculosis. There you are, breathing heavy from carrying over one-hundred pounds around a tight corner or down a flight of stairs. The remains of the decedent in your arms are continuously being jostled and manipulated to accommodate your fatigue and the physical obstacles that you are encountering. The odds are that there is some air left in the lungs of the decedent that you are moving, and all of the movement that the dead body is going through will undoubtedly expel some amount of that air out of their lungs, you have then been exposed. Then ask yourself, "How many people will be breathing the same air as me?"

Can you do all that and still play office politics?

As if dealing with grieving families and the stress of pulling off the "perfect" funerals on a daily basis isn't enough, every office setting has office politics. Truth be told, it was office politics that wore me down and burned me out of the business.

While working for a corporate company I had the misfortune of working under a manager who truly could not have cared less about the quality of service provided to the families that we served. He essentially used the funeral home as a slush fund for him and his family. He owned his own home, yet he used rental properties owned by the business to house his families. He employed family members and paid them for services never received. He employed the wife of his best friend as a secretary, in an effort to keep their extramarital affair hidden. He used company vehicles for all of his personal business, and since he was a salary employee, he would try to limit his workday to a couple of hours if he even showed up at all. I documented his work attendance for several months; he did not show up to work for a span of twenty-three days.

If you are wondering, yes, I did report this behavior to upper management. It was then that I lost interest in working for this funeral service provider ever again. It turns out that the person that I reported the incidents to also had several similar skeletons in his closet that were known to the employee I reported, but few others. The member of upper management strongly rebuked my supervisor, and the following month sent him a bonus check.

The services that were being offered to the public became sub-standard, members of the local clergy dreaded working with our firm and no-one that should have cared did. Our chapel had a full time staff of four, we served over two hundred families a year, and due to the office politics our staff routinely consisted of two employees. The office manager and I did our best to serve the community, while the location manager and the secretary were busy servicing one another.

The funeral business is an emotionally draining environment. If you are contemplating a career in the mortuary industry, make sure that your temperament allows you to "leave" everything at the office. One couple that I know, both work at the same funeral home, they found themselves frequently talking about work while they were at home, in an effort to curtail this habit, they decided to place a one dollar fine on one another whenever a conversation about work would begin. The one-dollar fine proved to be too steep; the couple had to reduce the fine to a quarter until the habit became less entrenched.

Please know that the funeral business is a "service" industry. Service is the only "item" that is individual to you. A casket may be purchased from many providers, including Costco or internet-based stores, however, your professionalism and your attitude towards service are unique and distinct. Make certain that the service that you provide is the best that it can be, while many people in this modern world are married multiple times, it is still true that you only have one funeral.

Chapter Three

What is learned in

mortuary college?

Just like any other major or emphasis of study at the higher education level, Mortuary Science encompasses a wide breath of study. Mortuary Science education subjects may be broken down into four categories: General Education, Health Sciences, the topics of Funeral Practices and Directing as well as Small Business Management.

General Education

All accredited mortuary colleges offering Associate and Bachelor Degrees require General Education courses as part of their curriculum. These courses are, for the most part, universal subjects that are required of all students seeking degrees from any college or university. Typically students will be required to take at least one class each in the following subject matter, History, English, Math, Foreign Language and/ or another Fine Art. However, some students may be required to take additional "pre-requisite" classes in order to ensure proficiency in future course work. Common areas where you might have classes required as a pre-requisite are Math, English and Science. It does you no favor as a student to place you into Algebra if you are stumped by fractions. Likewise, if you are not that proficient in writing, it is best to strengthen your skills before being required to compile a ten-page report on Modern Embalming in the Post Civil War Era.

Health Science Courses

Due to the fact that many of the Mortuary Science Programs are run by Community Colleges and Public Universities, there is often a co-mingling of Mortuary Science students with other Health Care Professional students, such as nursing students. In these co-mingled programs the specialized focus of applied science for the embalmer is lost. Generalized science courses of anatomy, pathology, microbiology, chemistry and communicable disease are required by nearly every public college mortuary science program.

On the other hand a private mortuary college student population is singularly focused on the sanitizing and safe disposition of the dead human body. A "true" mortuary college is able to tailor the curriculum to include the generalized curriculum requirement as well as the more specific information needed to keep their students safe from communicable disease and to prevent postmortem complications, such as decomposition, from ruining a family's opportunity to complete their funeral services in accordance with their traditions.

Funeral Practices and Directing

Everyday in our life we see professionals who specialize in a certain discipline within their chosen vocation. The medical field is broken down into an infinite number of specialty practices; podiatrist, pediatrics, cardiologist, internal medicine, dermatologist, proctologist, surgeons and countless other concentrations can be found. Gone are the days of having a family attorney. We now see family law, criminal law, trial lawyers, personal injury lawyers, business law specialists, intellectual property lawyers and countless other focuses within the legal community. To be a little more nostalgic, food service industries have seen a shift from the Diner to a focus of cuisine or service. Fast food of all varieties, coffee houses, organic culinary specialists and every fare imaginable is now for sale somewhere.

This is rarely the case with funeral service providers. Due to the fact that American cities are becoming more diverse places to live, so to are the funeral traditions practiced within that community. Since it wouldn't make very much business sense in most communities to have a number of "boutique" funeral providers to serve the needs of every minority represented in any given city, it makes much more sense to have the mortician be well versed in the funeral traditions of the community she serves. It should be noted that "boutique" funeral homes are not uncommon in certain areas of the United States. In the northeast, as well as the south, small firms assist twenty five to sixty families a year. These firms are generally recognized as the service providers for a particular religion or race.

Imagine a city of eighty thousand people. You can be certain that you will have members of the community who are Mormons, Catholics, Protestant, Buddhist, Jewish, Unitarian and non-religious people. You can also be certain that you will serve a very vast population of races and nationalities. The immigrant population has grown everywhere in the United States. With a large number of immigrants from Central and South America, the Middle East, South East Asia and the former Soviet Republics. A great deal of the curriculum taught in mortuary colleges involves the funeral and burial traditions of many cultures.

Business Management

Just like any professional practice the mortuary is a business. The purpose of any business is to make money. Please note that making money is not dishonest or evil. As a matter of fact, businesses make money solely based on the fact that they provide a good or a service that you cannot or will not provide for yourself. The only service that a funeral home provides that you most likely are not able to do, is the embalming of the dead human body.

Part of the mortuary college curriculum involves the teaching of skills needed to manage and operate a business on a day-to-day basis. Business law courses are required to teach students about federal and state statutes that must be complied with when dealing with families that they serve, the employees who work for them and other regulations set forth by OSHA and other various government agencies including State Mortuary and Cemetery Boards.

Classes that focus on business operations include merchandising, accounting, marketing, brand management and other general business courses. These classes vary from college to college and differ greatly based on if the institution offering the course is a public or private institution. Not many public community colleges offer courses strictly focused on the merchandising of caskets, urns and other death care industry specific products.

How to Select a Mortuary College

There are currently fifty-four mortuary colleges in the United States. Some are private institutions of higher education, others are programs operated by and on the campuses of public universities and community colleges. While it is true that you get out of education what you put into, the vehicle used for learning is a critical component in the educational equation.

When I decided to attend mortuary college, I was living in the Central Valley of California. At the time there were only two mortuary science programs located in California. Cypress Community College, located in Orange County and San Francisco College of Mortuary Science. Both schools offered similar scholastic programs, but that is where the similarities ended.

At that time, I knew graduates and dropouts from both programs. I quizzed them and questioned them as to what they felt were the pros and cons of each institution. Besides hearing the standard "be true to your school" rhetoric, most people were very forthcoming on why they made the decision they made and, surprisingly enough, it was the money. With little deviation, most people I spoke with would have preferred to attend the private school in San Francisco, however, the cost was too great.

At that time, there were many activities and programs offered to students attending school at Cypress which were not offered to the students of the San Francisco College of Mortuary Science. However, few if any bore a direct impact on the Mortuary Science Program. Cypress College is a Junior College that offered extra-curricular activities; sports, drama and expanded scholastic programs such as computer science and aviation programs. A few people that I spoke with who attended Cypress enjoyed the liberty of being able to take in a greater variety of elective courses. However, the majority of people wanted to complete the program in the shortest amount of time and really didn't show an interest in what other scholastic programs or extracurricular activities were offered. I assure you that few mortuary college students have selected their school by whether or not they could be the starting second baseman. It is totally up to you as the student to decide what "exactly" you are looking for in a mortuary science program.

Since my graduation from the San Francisco College of Mortuary Science, the school has been moved to Sacramento and is now part of the American River Community College system. This move and restructuring negates the reasoning behind my decision to attend the San Francisco College of Mortuary Science.

At the time I'd selected to attend school in San Francisco, that college was the only program in the country operating its own daily, open to the public, funeral home. Students would assist the families in funeral arrangements, embalm, dress and casket the deceased, as well as direct funeral services in our chapel. The fact that students went through this type of training made a serious impact on all students. For those of us who have ever "role played" at work or at school, you realize the difference between "acting" and "doing".

Selecting a Mortuary College is just like selecting a course of study at any other college. Considerations must be made for a programs reputation, academic success, location and quality of facility and the experience and education of the teaching staff. This information should be available from the course catalogs and over the phone with a program counselor. If you truly want an independent assessment of a programs staff and curriculum quality, find out what the Pass/Fail rate is for the previous years students, when they take the National Funeral Board Exam.

The National Funeral Board Exam is a true barometer of a programs quality. The International Conference of Funeral Service Examining Boards, Inc. administers the exam. The exam is currently broken down into two sections; an Art Section and a Science Section. The Art Section has seven subsets that are evaluated, the number of questions for this section are broken down as follows: Sociology/Funeral Service History -18 items, Psychology - 21 items, Funeral Directing - 27 items, Business Law - 18 items, Funeral Service Law - 24 items, Funeral Service Merchandising - 18 items, Accounting/Computers - 24 items and this section also contains 20 pretest items.

The Science Section of the exam is broken down into six subsets; subjects and the number of questions evaluated are as follows: Embalming - 42 items, Restorative Art - 42 items, Microbiology - 15 items, Pathology - 24 items, Chemistry - 12 items, Anatomy - 15 items and this section also contains 20 pretest items.

The National Funeral Board exam is an exhausting exam to take. The exam is time tested and begins at 8a.m. and typically ends at 5p.m. with a break between sections for lunch. For those who are wondering, yes, I did pass the National Funeral Board Exam on my first attempt.

There are other important things to consider when selecting a mortuary college, such as, how will the units earned transfer to another school or university? I had a problem with this myself. I transferred my unit credits to Chapman University and had little to no problem having them accepted; however, my Grade Point Average (GPA) was lower upon transfer due to the stringent grading scale of San Francisco College of Mortuary Science. The college had a grading scale of 70-74% is equal to a D, 75 – 84% is equal to a C, 85-94% is equal to a B and 95% and above earns you the A grade. However, when my GPA was transferred, it was done so as a "straight across" transfer. This didn't stop me from earning my degree in the same amount of time, as I would have expected, however, it made academic honors more difficult to achieve.

Also be aware of who owns your school. If you attend a community college, that is an easy way to see if you will obtain an unbiased quality education. However, if your college is owned or heavily sponsored by a corporate entity such as a corporate funeral service provider, casket company, or embalming chemical company you may want to ask further questions about teaching techniques and products being utilized in your education. Just like in school, one must do their homework when selecting a school.

Chapter Four

How do you embalm a body?

I have been asked countless times, "Is it hard to embalm a body?" Since no two bodies are exactly the same, that question becomes a very difficult one to answer. Doctors perform "routine" appendectomies on a daily basis, however I wouldn't describe that as an "easy" procedure, just routine. Embalming is very similar to any "routine" medical procedure, each involves risk to self and each offers up unique challenges to be overcome.

Traditionally the human scale for determining if a task is difficult, or not, is rather simple, "Are WE able to do it?" I would consider running a six-minute mile, rebuilding a transmission, sculpting anything that would resemble art or correctly completing anything more mathematically challenging than a simple polynomial as a "difficult" task. However, if you are properly trained and educated and you are willing to invest enough time into the "hands on" experience, you can become proficient in just about anything.

Think about it. Do you consider the people who change your brakes and balance your tires to be intellectually superior to you? Would you be able to mix a batch of concrete without using a bag of "premix"? Can you bake a cake from scratch? Are you able to sew an article of clothing that you would actually wear in public? If you cannot, I am certain that you could learn to do any of or all of the tasks sited. All you would need is training. This is true with every vocation.

The embalming process and the steps that you would follow would vary from person to person, depending on the challenges that each unique case would present with. An elderly person, who died of natural causes quietly in their sleep, while lying on their back, would be a relatively simple case and present few complications. However, if the same person had a disease that caused "jaundice" skin tones, the approach an embalmer would take in the embalming process may significantly change as a result. The same could be said for the person who died in a traumatic accident. The challenges presented in a case with multiple open injuries and lacerations, who may present with significant bruising and localized swelling will most certainly create challenges that will take much more time and focus to treat.

Tools Required

The tools of embalming are simple medical instruments. An embalmer on any case will need: a scalpel or pair of surgical scissors, two aneurysm needles, ligature, suture needle and an embalming machine.

Other tools and products are used during the embalming process, and much of it comes down to the individual embalmers personal preferences. Take for example that I prefer not to use a scalpel. There is a much greater risk to the embalmer who uses one. As a matter of fact, I know an embalmer, (he and I worked at the same mortuary and we attended mortuary college together) who accidentally dropped the scalpel from the embalming table. During its descent toward the ground the blade became stuck in his leg above the knee. The infection that raged for months had to be battled with forms of "chemo" therapy, and finally after months of aggressive medical treatment the decision was made that they would need to amputate his leg above the knee. In my opinion, the risk a scalpel brings to the equation outweighs the embalmers need for one.

A scalpel or pair of surgical scissors is utilized in making the necessary incisions to perform the embalming procedure. The number of incision points will vary in number from case to case, usually ranging from one to six. The same instrument may also be used to size ligature to lengths needed.

Ligature is a fancy way of saying string. We're not talking about the "needle and thread" string used in your home sewing kit. The ligature used by the embalmer is typically made of thick cotton string that is then coated in wax. The reasoning for the wax coating is simple, it prevents the "wicking" effect that would draw moister from within the body through the ligature used for closing incision points and possibly to a place where it could ruin clothing or stain the interior of a casket.

For every primary incision point, an incision where both a vein and an artery will be raised, five pieces of ligature will be needed. Ligature will be used to "tie off" both ends on the vein and the artery opened and used for the embalming process. The last remaining length of ligature will be used for the closing of the incision point.

The embalmer will use aneurysm needles when "raising", or locating the veins and arteries needed to complete the embalming process. The aneurysm needles are very helpful in completing many tasks. An embalmer will use them to move fascia (the connective tissue surrounding and securing blood vessels) in their effort to expose the walls of the vessels. The embalmer may also wish to use the aneurysm needle to "loop" the needed ligatures around the vessels that will be opened and utilized during the process.

Embalming Machine:

An embalming machine is a tank, generally of three gallons in size with a motorized pump that is connected to the body by a hose that will be inserted into an artery. The tank will hold the mixture commonly referred to as embalming fluid. Also part of this tank includes two meters and valves that allow the embalmer to control both the pressure and the rate of flow of the embalming fluid. While a machine is utilized in delivering the "embalming fluid" to the body, the body being embalmed actually is the most helpful link in the system.

When "embalming fluid" is introduced into an artery the embalming machine may be dictating the amount of pressure and the amount of fluid being sent, however, the human arterial system receives the fluid, and treats it just as it would the blood that it normally shuttles through the body. Arteries, capillaries and veins exchange the body's own natural supply of fluids with the preserving fluid mixed by the embalmer. Due to the body's "cooperative" part in the embalming process, much of "how difficult" an embalming can be is related to the condition of the body.

Many medical conditions can "disrupt" or add complications to the embalming process. If a person has a condition that results in the retention of a great deal of water, this can lead to either swelling, or having the "embalming fluid" diluted within the body, leading to localized areas of decomposition. Poor circulation may also lead to complications in the embalming process. If the body has a difficult time distributing its own fluids, there is a better than average chance that the body will have a difficult time distributing the embalming fluid thoroughly. This will, at times, require that an embalmer use multiple injection sites.

Embalming Fluid:

Just like any other branded product, there is a wide selection of embalming fluids that an embalmer may select from. Some of the major brands of embalming fluid include Dodge, Pierce and Champion fluids. Each brand that I have mentioned offers a wide variety of fluids and is a respected brand within the industry. There are other fluid companies and just because I have not mentioned them should not lead anyone to believe that the products they provide is of an inferior quality. General Motors sells more cars a year than Rolls Royce, that doesn't necessarily mean that the products offered by GM are of superior quality.

Embalming fluid companies spend a great deal of time and money in an effort to aid the embalmer in their job. Companies offer products that "condition" the arteries. The "pre-injection" products are mixed and injected prior to the embalming process. The goal of these products is to dilate the vessels, dissolve blood clots and aid in the clearing of any skin discoloration that may be present.

"Co-injections" can be mixed with primary fluids, and have similar traits as "pre-injections", but may also include additional cosmetic dyes. The dyes are introduced to the body in an effort to help the embalmer obtain a more "natural" skin tone as well give an embalmer an added tool of being able to physically track the distribution of fluid to the tissues. As the tissue changes color an embalmer will be able to more easily identify if an area of tissue is not receiving an adequate amount of embalming fluid.

While there are several embalming fluids and additives available to the embalmer, it is still up to the embalmer to review each individual decedent and recognize the challenges of each one on a case-by-case basis and mix the appropriate amounts of arterial conditioner, dyes and preservative fluids. While an embalmer may utilize similar percentages per tank of fluid, each case is embalmed with a fluid that the embalmer has determined to be the most advantageous on an individual basis.

Step-By-Step Guide

After placing a decedent on an embalming table the embalmer will due a thorough evaluation of the body. The embalmer will first remove any and all articles of clothing, taking care to evaluate the entire body for any open tissue (bed sores, rashes and cuts) that may need to be treated. The skin itself will also be thoroughly evaluated, looking for dehydration, water retention, discoloration or areas of "skin slip". Skin slip is a skin condition that often-time leads to painful "tears" in the skin in elderly people. It may be compared to "chap" skin, however, this condition presents areas of concern for the embalmer. If an area of skin is torn and remains untreated, it may result in a situation where it may "leak" (if the person were still alive we'd say bleed) and ruin clothing or stain the interior of their casket.

After the embalmer has removed all articles of clothing, they will "pose the decedents features. The embalmer will cover the eyes with a flesh colored "eye cap" (which looks a lot like larger contact lenses) and then they will place the eyelids over the eye cap. Eyelid placement in itself is an art form. If not done properly the eye expression could look like someone squinting or like someone is trying to "sneak a peek" without opening his or her eyes. After the eyelids have been closed and posed, the embalmer will close and pose the mouth of the deceased.

The most common way to pose the mouth is by using an "injector needle". The injector needle is an industry specific tool. A needle injector acts on the same principals of a rivet. Two small, pointy spike are placed in the gum line, one in the upper gums just below the nose and the second being place directly below the other in the lower gum line. Attached to the injector needle is a wire, some use stainless steel others use brass, I have used both and have no preference of one over the other. After the needle injector is securely in place an embalmer will use the attached wires to secure the mouth in a closed position. Once again the embalmer must take care in posing facial features. If the mouth is closed too tightly, the deceased may appear to be gritting his or her teeth. If the mouth is too loosely posed, it may look to others as if the deceased are about to say something. In either case, the appearance of the deceased "just won't look right".

In some instances a "mouth former" is required. A mouth former is a thin piece of plastic that helps create the appearance of a natural "teeth" line. If a person has no teeth and dentures can't be found, or in a case where the front teeth are very "prominent' and may protrude past the lips, a mouth former may be used to provide a more uniform look to a mouth. Whatever the case, an embalmer must take great care in posing facial features. No matter how great the embalming of tissue may be, if the face doesn't look natural, the embalmer has failed.

After the facial features have been posed the embalmer will then lightly spray the body or otherwise apply a topical disinfectant. It is at this point that the embalmer may begin to bathe the body. Part of the embalming process is the disinfecting of the remains. Embalmers will then mix their chemical solutions for the embalming process. While the tank of fluids is mixing in the embalming machine, the embalmer will begin to raise the vessels needed during the embalming process. Just above the collar bone on the deceased's right side an incision will be made. Through this small, usually one to two inch incision the embalmer will raise both the common carotid artery and the jugular vein. A tube connecting the embalming machine to the deceased is placed in the common carotid. A "drainage tube" is then placed in the jugular vein. The drainage tube is not attached to a piece of equipment, however, it will lead to a drain or sump of some sort to dispose of any fluids that may be expelled from the body during the embalming process.

At this point it would be common for an embalmer to begin the injection of embalming fluid by selecting the rate of flow and the pounds per square inch pressure that he or she feels is the most appropriate. While the embalming machine does its job, the embalmer continues the process of disinfecting the body by shampooing the hair and bathing the body with an anti-microbial/anti-bacterial soap. This process is also a vital part of the embalming process. The "massaging" of the tissue during the bathing process tends to help the embalming fluid penetrate any clots that may have formed in capillaries and also helps significantly in the process of clearing any post mortem staining.

A post mortem stain can simply be defined as the dark discoloration that occurs when blood settles to the lowest points in the dead body. This naturally occurring discoloration creates little problem if the deceased is quickly embalmed after death or spent its post mortem hours on its back. However, if a person died after collapsing face first on a floor or quietly died while sleeping on their side, not to be found for a few hours, the post mortem staining to areas like the ears, face and hands will create more difficult areas for the embalmer to treat.

At the conclusion of the arterial embalming process, the embalmer must perform the process of treating the thoracic and abdominal cavities. This process is essential to the proper preservation of remains and also is crucial in controlling situations where "purging" may be a problem.

Purging is just as unpleasant as it sounds. The thoracic and abdominal cavities are filled with some amount of fluids. Food or drinks consumed prior to death, fluid that had built up in the lungs during respiratory failure, or any number of medical conditions may have caused a build up of fluids.

After death the body has no ability to control the muscles that are responsible for keeping bodily fluids inside the body. "Purge" is the event by which these types of fluids escape the body via the mouth or nose.

An embalmer tries to prevent this from happening, with every bit of our "know how". Very few events can alarm a family or ruin a public viewing like a purging decedent. To prevent the "purge" problem, embalmers will employ a trocar aspirator to remove gases and fluids from the abdominal and thoracic cavities and then using the same trocar that has been disinfected to add an embalming fluid commonly called "cavity fluid". Cavity fluid is a very strong embalming fluid, and is generally free of dyes and perfumes.

That's embalming in a "nut-shell"; and there are still a number of activities that an embalmer must do prior to any one seeing their loved one. Some of those activities include, doing their hair and make-up, dressing them, placing them in their casket and staging the visitation room with the flowers and lighting.

Chapter Five

Should I pre-arrange my funeral?

There are many forms of "Pre-Arranged" funerals and a plethora of companies that support them. Read this chapter and I'll show you how to save hundreds, if not hundreds of thousands of dollars, on your final arrangements. I will also teach you some very important topics to cover with your estate attorney. Since I am not an attorney, and I have never played one on TV, do not consider my opinions as legal advice. These are my suggestions to you, and you may want to talk them over with your attorney.

I have yet to find a funeral home in America that does not offer prepaid funeral plans. One might be out there, but I have not found it yet. Pre-paid funerals are, in my opinion, an insane way that funeral homes attempt to build their business. No independent market research has ever been conducted on the subject, but I am willing to bet that over 95% of those who selected a funeral home to pre-arrange with would have made arrangements with that same business at the time of need.

The notion of pre-paid goods and services, being offered on indeterminate terms without direct control of operating cost or product availability is utter madness. Can you imagine going into your local Lexus dealer and paying on a car over the next ten years that you're not going to take delivery of for thirty more years? How much have cars gone up in price over the last forty years? How much control has the auto industry had over cost increases? Imagine, funeral homes are happy to make this poor business decision every day of the week.

Funeral homes ought to get wise to the losses they're taking, and you should take advantage of their stupidity. Not only are they locking in a lower price, they also limit their ability to collect on "up-sales" because families can rely on "We'll just do what Mom wanted." Pre-need arrangements block emotional purchases. This is a good thing for the consumer, and a bad thing for the mortuary business. After all, when the funeral home gets cash strapped, it's not like they can have a sidewalk sale. Mortuaries need to be profitable, like ALL businesses, and it is foolish for them to lock in a lower average sale. However, you know the saying about a fool and his money.

Currently, Service Corp. International is building their brand with a national campaign, "Dignity Memorial". You most likely have seen their advertisements or heard their radio spots. To be honest with you, "Dignity Memorial" is a much better brand building image than "McDeath". Believe it or not, their size is your advantage.

Service Corp. has cemeteries and funeral homes in nearly every state. They, in their efforts to grow market share, offer pre-arranged funeral and cemetery plans. If you work their system right you can save a fortune. With a marketing and sales plan that lacks wisdom, they allow consumers to purchase services and property at one location and "if needed" will transfer it to another location. How foolish!

For example, a consumer could buy a "Private Family Garden" in a medium size market, similar to Tulsa, OK, for the price of $16,000. The owner could then turn around and transfer that purchase, item for item – not dollar for dollar, to a prime market, like Los Angeles, San Francisco, New York, Chicago or Seattle. By doing this the consumer could save $160,000.

Additionally, prices at individual mortuaries vary, sometimes greatly. Imagine purchasing a funeral plan at a mortuary located in Tulare, CA for $4,300 and then transferring it to San Diego where the same services and products typically cost the consumer double.

Additionally, caskets are a major percentage of the overall funeral home bill. There are several casket companies. Batesville Caskets is the top of the heap with the largest market share in the industry. They also have one of the highest wholesale prices. In my opinion, they make a superior product, however, you are going to pay for it. If you want to save money, and you notice that your local funeral home only carries Batesville Casket, ask your Funeral Director to provide you options from another company. There are dozens of regional casket suppliers; and if you are a budget minded shopper, I would suggest that you look at another national company, like York Caskets, as a less costly alternative to Batesville Caskets.

While the pre-payment of your final expenses is a nice thing to do for your family, there could be a real advantage to talking it over with your estate planning attorney. Especially if you need to unload assets to qualify for a government run health care plan or long term nursing home care.

In some instances you can pre-pay up to $10,000 toward burial expenses and not have it count against your assets in the qualification process. Then discuss the option of paying the max and then having your next of kin "alter" the services provided after the death has occurred. More than once I have seen a family change the final arrangement from a full traditional burial to a direct disposition and pocket the difference – TAX FREE! Talk it over with your attorney.

I encourage everyone, especially anyone owning anything worth more than $10,000 to consult with an estate planning attorney to prevent the need to enter into probate to settle your estate. Probate costs can be tens of thousands of dollars, and if that is all you have, then you have effectively left your estate to the local attorney. Do yourself and your family a favor and consult with a qualified estate attorney before it's too late, especially if you have young children!

We all recall the famous case in Florida of a woman who was in a vegetative state for years. Not only were the family members at odds, pitting husband against parents, but also Congress and the Courts offered their opinions and crafted new law. Do yourself and your family a favor and create an Advanced Health Care Directive or Living Will.

They are cheap to set up, and court battles are expensive to wage. Everyone over the age of eighteen should have an Advanced Healthcare Directive. Honestly ask yourself, if I am seriously injured in a car accident do I want my family to be asked about life support options, organ donation options, or other anatomical gifts?

Pre-arrangement if worked properly can be a financial advantage for consumers. However, not every pre-need plan is a good one. The Forethought Company is one of the most respected names in the business, and many funeral homes will keep your pre-need funds in a trust. Be a smart consumer and make sure you are working with a reputable company.

Chapter Six

Cremation: Does it REALLY cost less?

The short answer is, no. What is the difference between burial and cremation? The answer is simple; it is where the body of the deceased is driven after the services. Direct burial is like direct cremation except instead of turning right at the cemetery gates, the mortician turns left to continue on to the crematory.

As a Funeral Director, I have witnessed families select cremation options that far exceed the average burial options. With cremation you can still have a funeral, prior to cremation. There is also the option of a memorial service with or without the cremated remains present. A service with the cremated remains present would of course take place after the cremation process.

Just as you see with traditional earth burial, every option of caskets including metal caskets can be selected by a family selecting the cremation option. However, I would suggest not purchasing a metal casket. A metal casket will leave far more debris that will need to be separated from the cremated remains at the end of the cremation process.

I mentioned Batesville Casket Company previously, they, as a company, were slow to embrace the cremation consumer and the entire product lines which service that segment of the market. However, now they not only have embraced the cremation market, they are revolutionizing the market with their "Options" line.

Their Cremation Casket line offers an environmentally friendly process from start to finish, minimizing the amount of metal hardware used as well as water based stains and coatings, which limits the amount of pollution (i.e. smoke) that occurs during the cremation process. The line of urns that are offered under their Options brand provides beautiful products at every price point. Additionally, they offer incredibly eco-friendly scattering urns that dissolve in water, or provide soil enriching nutrients for earth burial. Batesville has spent a great deal of time, energy, and money to develop a comprehensive line that meets the need of nearly every consumer.

Cost of either burial or cremation is up to the consumer. There are Memorial Association and other Societies that will offer you direct cremations at a minimal cost, usually under $1,000. However, you always get what you pay for, and with that being said, you should also only pay for what you need. However, there are just as many, if not more, decisions that need to be made when cremation has been selected as the method of final disposition.

When making final arrangements and selecting products, when opting for cremation, the process is actually longer not shorter and certainly not easier. In all actuality, it becomes a more involved process focused on attention to detail.

To begin with, there are multiple cremation authorization forms, due to the fact that one can always disinter an individual whose been buried, but you cannot undo the cremation process. There are also a greater number of products required in the cremation process; they include the selection of the legally required cremation container (i.e. casket, coffin, or cardboard box), the selection of an urn, and the selection of a final disposition location (i.e. scattering garden, scattering at sea, or cemetery niche). I want to stress to you that cremation and burial can be nearly identical in price in some locations of the United States, especially for those served by District Cemeteries or for Veterans entitled to a burial plot in a National Cemetery.

I caution you though, please be deliberate and truly thoughtful about the final disposition of cremated remains. Death is not a time for arrogance. When I die, I am sure that my wife and son will care where my body is located, and if I live long enough my grandchildren may care. However, two generations from now I doubt they will give a wit about the location of my body. It seems that almost on a weekly basis funeral homes are contacted by a new home owner or tenant asking what they should do with the urn that they found stashed away in the back of a closet. View cremated remains as you should, as human remains; they eventually need a final resting place.

Chapter Seven

How can I save money?

You will not get a funeral for free, unless they really screw it up, and then again, it just proves the old saying that you get what you pay for. However, there are a number of ways to lower your funeral costs substantially. View this chapter as my helpful guide to assist you through the funeral arrangement process. These are tips and not "hard and fast" rules. Each situation and funeral home is different, but not so much so that these rules aren't going to save you money.

CASKETS HAVE A HUGE MARK-UP

Caskets aren't generally sold for any other purpose than to bury the dead. I have not seen one slaloming down the slopes or winning a soapbox derby. The market for caskets is generally limited to the number of deaths in your town, and with cremation rates on the rise, casket sales naturally are going to drop accordingly. Funeral homes have long built their business on casket sales. In today's economy funeral service providers must balance out single item profit margins to compete with wholesale clubs and e-sellers. If you are close to a Costco or have a trusted internet casket provider, use that fact to your advantage when negotiating the price of a casket. Yes, casket prices are negotiable, and so is nearly anything else that you will be charged for at the funeral home.

There is nothing morally wrong with saying: "I am not willing to pay the usual mark-up on that casket. I am willing to pay you $500 over what you pay for it, or you'll lose the casket sale." Very few businesses are going to let $500 just walk out the door. A move like this can save you thousands. For example, at one funeral home that I worked for we would buy a casket that we paid $675 wholesale for and we would then turn around and retail that same casket for $2,195. So, even on a lower end casket your savings is substantial. However, don't try this on a casket under $1,000. Lower the number to $250 over invoice, or your mortician may laugh at your willingness to pay him more than his usual mark-up.

Caskets are not usually marketing tools, however, a great deal of time, effort and market research is used to determine how to merchandise a casket and cremation selection room. The caskets (units) floored, the location where a particular unit is placed in a showroom, retail mark-up and showroom carpet and paint colors have been strategically plotted to take as much advantage as possible of the consumers inexperience and emotional needs.

This is how I worked my casket sale - I would walk the family to the door, and just before opening it I would say:

"In our casket selection room you'll find a wide variety of caskets. You'll find both wood and metal caskets. The metal caskets are displayed by category. You'll find semi-precious metals such as bronze, copper and stainless steel. These are the more expensive caskets in the showroom. Please keep in mind that if you are interested in a casket possessing the qualities of the semi-precious metals, such as protection from rust or velvet interior, please let me know, and I can prepare photos of other options currently not shown in the selection room at this time."

I would then open the door, and as I walked the family in I would show them briefly, the caskets I had just described. I would then continue to walk them to the standard steel caskets, and I would then tell them:

"Here you will find our standard steel caskets; you'll see that some are 20 gauge, some 18 gauge and a few of them are even 16 gauge. As you know, steel like thread, is gauged so that the lower the number the thicker the steel."

I would then walk to a casket and say: "Before I leave and give you your privacy to discuss amongst yourself, I want to go over a few of the features of our caskets."

I would then show them the Memory Drawer, the Memorial Tube, the locking mechanism and the rubber gasket that "helps to protect against the elements". I would then say:

"There are two types of materials used for casket interiors, the first being a crepe material", and I would invite them to touch it. I would then say, "The second material is velvet, as you can feel the velvet is a softer material and warmer to the touch."

I would then say, "And one last thing before I leave the room, in this area of the showroom is where we have our wood caskets. You'll see that they range in price depending on wood variety such as mahogany, cherry or pine and the woodworking details. Some are very simple and some are very ornate. If you have any questions, I'll be in the hall. Just open the door and I'll be happy to assist you, or answer any questions you may have. Oh, and please don't try to close any of the caskets without my help; they are equipped with locking hinges that may become damaged if not closed properly."

That may sound like a mouth full, however, there was not one wasted breath or movement and I am certain to have maximized my sale. Did you spot the subtle, or not so subtle, use of verbiage to direct the consumer? Let's do a quick walk through of why I did and said what I did.

In explaining about semi-precious metal caskets, I set up a price point. "Semi-precious" is a fancy way of saying "expensive". By walking you through the selling points, I also made "rust" an issue. That's not a big deal in Los Angeles, however, in Eugene, Oregon or Florida, you bet that statement carries some mental imagery. I then set a "luxury" tone around the velvet interior; imagine the difference is akin to a cloth or leather sofa, one sounds more luxurious. I then left the conversation with "if interested" to immediately determine how much you have planned on spending. Very few casket sales are of this variety of casket, and we funeral service providers know it. In all actuality our mark-up on a bronze, copper or stainless steel casket is much lower than that of a "standard steel" casket.

"Standard Steel" is my favorite buyer's direction of all. By classifying something as "standard" I'm essentially saying that anything less than this and you are being cheap. Also, by using this term I give an indication that this is what most people buy. I further direct the consumer to touch the interiors. Who doesn't think that velvet feels wonderful, regardless of what the other material it is being compared to is? Your comfortable cotton bed linens can't compare, however, you sleep on them each night. And yet I've convinced you that Aunt Sally would rest for eternity more comfortably with a casket that has velvet interior.

Couple these "Standard", "Velvet" and "Gauge of Steel" and what have I just sold you? I sold you an 18 Gauge Steel Casket with a velvet interior that retails for about $3,200 to $3,700. How am I certain that it will be an 18 gauge steel casket? Because, it's in the middle, 20 gauge steel "seems" thin, and is there really a "need" for a 16 gauge steel?

If you walk into just about any casket selection room and count the caskets and walk to the exact middle of the room, you're going to find an 18 gauge steel casket with velvet interior. Consumers feel "safe" being in the middle. They don't want to "over pay" and they usually do not want to be considered "cheap".

What about the wood caskets you ask? Very good question - woods are less popular in most of the United States, and are a more expensive product to manufacture. Most places only carry a minimal selection of wood caskets. Wood caskets are generally more expensive than metal caskets, and less sought after by consumers. However, a good rule to follow, never buy the "pine box" that Uncle Lou always talked about while camping. The pine caskets generally will have the highest mark-up, because twice a year some family comes in and says "Dad always said just burry me in an old pine box."

AUTOMOBILES

The livery vehicles of a funeral home are often over priced and unneeded. You really only need one car, and that's the one that will transport the casket during the service. You will undoubtedly be asked about a "Flower Car". Unless you have a "wall" of flowers, the flowers can be transported with the casket in the coach/hearse. Additionally, most funeral homes don't want to accept responsibility for damaging flowers while transporting them, so they'll use the flower car for you free of charge.

Additionally, ask yourself what is important to you. Do you really need to spend a couple of hundred dollars on a pall bearer limo, or a family limo? If you don't need them, don't ask for them. Also, ask what year the cars are. If they say their fleet is a 1978 Lincoln Limo, definitely negotiate a lower price. How long do you think those cars have been paid for, and really how far are they taking you?

PRINTED MATERIALS

Do yourself a favor, and buy the Register Book and the Memorial Folders from your funeral home. You will not believe how many times I have seen a family try to save $15 and go to Kinko's to have the printing done, only to realize that they screwed up the spelling of a Pall Bearers name, or left something of great importance to them out entirely. If you notice an error at the funeral home, they can jump right on it and reprint them; however, Kinko's isn't as accommodating. Additionally, Kinko's will charge you for the second running, most funeral homes will not.

NEGOTIATIONS

All service fees and retail pricing are fair game for negotiating. However, I recommend that you pick your battles. Negotiate the big stuff, if you save a couple grand on the casket, don't be "that guy" trying to save the $15 on the memorial folders. Funeral homes are businesses; these businesses do not operate as a not-for-profit charity. Remember that and be respectful. While everything is negotiable, remember that the only reasons these businesses exist is because they are willing to do for you something that you either cannot or will not do for yourself. The funeral service provider is not a pirate or predator; they are, like so many of us, just trying to do their jobs.

With that being said, let me give you one last piece of negotiating advice; don't ask to meet with the manager or owner. The funeral director, or apprentice, is going to be much more empathetic or even sympathetic to your needs and circumstances; after all, they are negotiating with "house money". An owner sees his vacation being negotiated away, or a manager envisions a smaller bonus at the end of the year. It's tough to out negotiate a person who has just as much, if not more, at stake.

Chapter Eight

How to have the perfect funeral

To have the "perfect" funeral or memorial service, you must first realize who you are remembering. That being said, you also have to remember that a funeral is for the living and must meet the needs of those who are actually going to be attending and participating in the service.

It is common place for a man and a woman who have been married for nearly half a century to die only a few months apart from one another. This was the case in my family; it has been the case with many of the families of my friends, as well as the families that I have served. I tell you this to give you this warning: it generally is not a good idea to have the same Pastor, Eulogist or Minister officiate the funeral for the second spouse who officiated the service of the first spouse. It rarely gives the feeling of personalization that you sensed at the first funeral. The reason why I suggest this is because the fact of the matter is that most pastors and ministers give the same funeral time after time, regardless of whose funeral they are officiating. If you are Catholic, it does not matter who the priest is that performs the Mass of Christian Burial, the words are always the same, with exception of the biographical information shared with the congregation, and this information is often shared by a family member or close friend.

Often time's funerals feel too stuffy. There is no dress code required, unless there is one that is. Don't take that to mean that the next time you attend a funeral you should do so in shorts, a tank top and flip flops. I am referring to your freedom to plan the funeral you want for a loved one. Take the Funeral of John Belushi for example; his friend Dan Aykroyd not only wore black jeans and a leather jacket, but he led the funeral procession on his motorcycle. Mourners were then stunned by Dan at the church when he played the Ventures "2000-pound Bee" during the service. The shock wore off the congregation, and their memories of John came to mind and they then could truly appreciate the memories through the grief.

That being said, grief is an essential part of any funeral or memorial service. These services provide an appropriate place to grieve and show the emotions that you feel; to voice sadness at loss or anger at a life snuffed out all too soon. It is unhealthy to store these emotions for any length of time. I assure you, if you do not take the time to express these emotions, they will not leave; they will just look for an opportunity to find release. You will appear sane when crying at a funeral. People will think that you're nuts if you break into tears, ten years after your husband has died, while standing in the produce aisle because you suddenly remembered how long it's been since you've heard his voice tell you how great your melons are. You need a place to grieve; you need that community of support. You don't have to pay your funeral home to do it, but you need it all the same.

Furthermore, just like in real estate, a place for a funeral or memorial service comes down to "location, location, location". If you expect a large crowd, as often seen with public figures (small time or big time), school aged children, notable death (think local tragedy, school shooting, mass murder victim) or a person involved in several service organizations, remember to get a location large enough not only to fit the group of mourners, but also make sure the facility has ample parking. Remember that few people carpool to a funeral, most take time from work to attend, and they will often times drive alone. Please plan accordingly.

Also remember that you are still alive after the death of a friend or family member. When making funeral arrangements after a death that will always give you pain, not that all deaths won't, but the death of a grandparent is much different than the death of your 12 year old son; I strongly suggest that if you must plan a funeral for those who are closely related or dear friends, have the funeral at the funeral home. Countless times, if a funeral is held at a church, I have heard it said that survivors are unable to walk into the church or chapel without the memory of the funeral, or visualizing where the casket was located, or where they sat during the service or other memories coming to mind in vivid detail. It makes since to have the funeral at the funeral home; how often do you find yourself there otherwise?

When it comes to the service itself, own it! Do it your way. I have always gone by the mantra, "If it's not illegal, immoral and nobody gets hurt, we can do it." I have wheeled the motorcycle of the deceased to the front of the chapel to focus attention during a memorial service. I have delivered a casket (empty) to the home of a family so that a teenage artist could customize it as one last tribute to her father. I have led all night wakes and viewings to accommodate the religious needs of Buddhist, Orthodox Jews, and Gypsies. I did have that come back and bite me on the fleshy hind quarters once when at an all night Hmong service they slaughtered a calf in my chapel. That was really a learning experience, and after that I always went over the ground rules thoroughly.

When planning the service of a loved one, the obituary is a very important historical record. Grant it, many papers charge, and there are several that charge a lot, however, be certain that the obituary reflects the life that you are recording in black and white for the rest of history. There is so much more to a person than, loving husband and father, or avid fisherman or scratch golfer. Approach the obituary as a time capsule. Write the obituary as if you are writing it for that genealogist who is tracing back their history three generations from now. What makes that life special? Think of those things and write them down. Feel free to be creative; if your mother was the best stay at home mom in the world, write that she was a "Domestic Goddess" (There is a death certificate out there that I filed that has that listed as "occupation", which goes to prove that everyone has their price and that cost me a large bag of M&M's to a county clerk).

Remember the flowers!!! "In lieu of flowers" is my least favorite sentence starter, and I use it now to warn you. I understand wanting monetary donations to be made in the name of your loved one; charity is a good thing. However, you have to live up to your end of the bargain and buy the flowers. Nothing looks as awkward and out of sort as a funeral without flowers. This is especially true with a memorial service; people expect to see something at the front of the room. A chapel or hall is a large room, and it looks awfully lonely in them if there is nothing to catch your eye. If you're loved one was adamant that there be no flowers, then make sure you have something as the focal point of the service. I've used small fishing boats and fishing gear, or artwork created by the deceased to create an area to view in lieu of flowers. Just make sure that whatever you do leaves a pleasant memory picture with you, and reflects the memory of the person you are remembering. The display also has to be large enough to appreciate from even the very back of the room. Who really wants to sit in the first three rows of a funeral?

Music selections, whether live or on CD, are used at nearly every funeral and memorial service. While there are standards that are often used, such as "Amazing Grace" and "The Old Rugged Cross", feel free to use other favorites to celebrate the life of your loved one. I have heard Frank Sinatra's "My Way" at a number of funerals and at the funeral of Anna Nicole Smith they played "On the Wings of a

Dove". While you have the freedom to make whatever musical selections you wish, and not everyone is the same, be thoughtful with your selections. If your loved one is best summed up by the lyrics of an alternative music song or something a little harder, then I suggest that you reframe from AC/ DC's "Hells Bells" and opt for something more appropriate, like Ozzy Osborne's "Life Won't Wait". Remember, if the public is invited, you owe some duty of care to them for their lasting memory picture.

Size and strength matters, with that being said, do not expect seventy-five year old men to act as pall bearers. Do everyone a favor and make them "Honorary Pall Bearers". Get the young and the strong to act as pall bearers. The size of the pall bearers is not always what matters; the size of the deceased has a lot to do with how things are going to work out. If the deceased weighs just an order of biscuits and gravy short of 400 pounds, please have more than six pall bearers. The stairs of the church or the distance from the funeral coach to the grave site can seem to be unobtainable goals to the poor pall bearer having to lift and carry 100 lbs for a significant time and distance. Imagine having to carry a 90 lbs bag of concrete 100 yards and up ten steps without setting it down. Now imagine having to do that in the heat of July in a black wool suit.

The "Perfect Funeral" means something different to everyone. That's why it's you who has to take ownership of the service and make it your own. I have planned thousands of funerals and I've tried to make each one unique. However, the more involved the family was in the planning stage, the more they appreciated the results. I caution you though, don't try to "micro-manage" the funeral; please let the funeral home staff do their jobs. Additionally, you shouldn't feel like you've worked a funeral, just be thoughtful and involved during the funeral arrangement process.

Chapter Nine

How to select a funeral service provider

Just as all cars are not created equal, neither are all funeral service providers. At one end of the service spectrum there is Memorial Association and Societies that are membership based and cater to those clients needing or wanting an inexpensive, low to no frills form of final disposition. At the other end of the spectrum are "top tier" service providers who have the most updated facilities, a superior automobile fleet, and the highest end of caskets and other products.

Michael Jackson's funeral didn't cost over $1 million dollars because he could afford it and his family was gouged. His funeral bill became that large because of the services and products requested by the family equaled that sum total. His gold plated bronze casket, around the clock security, leather bound register books, thousands of dollars spent on flowers daily, and countless other unusual expenditure inflated the bill into the absurd stratosphere of seven figures.

However, on the other side of the coin, there are a number of organizations that are selling the $550 direct cremation special. Just to show you how absurdly cheap that is, let me walk you through what a customer will get for that. A person or maybe two will wake up in the middle of the night, drive to the place of death (house, hospital, traffic accident), then take the deceased to their holding facility. They'll prepare the death certificate, deliver it to, and pick it back up from, the doctor who is signing the certificate. Then they will prepare a disposition permit and have both the death certificate and disposition permit recorded with the county. Next, they provide you with the legally required cremation container and the urn. Finally, they will then drive the deceased to the crematory and then retrieve the cremated remains to deliver them to you. That $550 direct cremation is cheap at twice the price.

Somewhere between the million dollar funeral and the $550 direct cremation is where the majority of consumers will find themselves. How you go about selecting a mortuary is specific to your needs. The majority of funeral home business is "legacy" business. Consumers will often select the same funeral home as previous generations in their family have used. I strongly suggest you don't do this.

There are numerous questions a consumer may ponder prior to selecting a funeral service provider. After all, you could end up spending thousands of dollars. Consumers must think. What is important to you? Do you know who owns your local funeral home? Do you care? Do you prefer to shop local? Aren't all "service" jobs equal to shopping local? Which funeral home has a better reputation? Which funeral home knows the most about your needs (religious, etc.)? Do you know their prices? Do you even know where they are going to keep the body of your loved one prior to the funeral? Is it at their facility in your town, or at a central location that serves several locations?

There is no "right" way to select a funeral service provider; however, there are numerous wrong ways. Going by, "That's where we had Aunt Sally's service", is one of the wrong ways. Be a savvy consumer; use your mind. Do you have Cadillac taste and a Kia budget? Shop around and look for those features that are important to you. Is there a new funeral home in town? Have you been in to see the interiors of these businesses? Have they not been updated since 1973?

In order to make the right choice you must arm yourself with answers to those questions that are important to you and your family. I would suggest that you periodically walk into your local funeral home and ask for the "General Price List"; they are required by law to provide you with a copy. If you want, ask if they can show you around. Look at the staff; judge their service style and attitude. Look over the facility; discover if their furniture is just whicker that has been spray painted or if the place looks clean and kept up. I believe that by doing this you will be able to determine who you like better, what facility is more to your liking, whose prices are within your budget, and ultimately who you will trust to take care of you in your time of need.

When selecting a funeral service provider, aside from pricing and facility maintenance, service and staff personality are important. I have long thought that I knew what funeral home I would select to provide services for my family when the need arises. However, lately my thoughts have changed, and I know for certain that if my three year old son has anything to say in the matter he would select differently than I thought I would have just last year.

Recently I started walking several miles a day to help maintain my general health; my son frequently makes the trip with me, hoisted upon my shoulders. I, of course, incorporated the local cemetery into our walk. After several days of this new routine, we started to make friends with the staff of the cemetery and the onsite mortuary. During the course of our daily walks a very kind, grandmotherly, woman started to come out and greet us. And to my son's delight, she would routinely bring him out a fresh baked chocolate chip cookie; and to my relief she would provide me with a cool bottle of water. My son now looks forward to our walks through the cemetery and past the office. He doesn't always take the cookie when it is offered, however, he is always happy to see his kind friend who offers them.

This woman who was being genuinely friendly and who probably loved seeing the joy in a little boy's eye, not only has won over generations of business, but did so by creating positive memory pictures within my son and me. Those in the funeral business should think about this. Could you imagine a place my son would rather have me buried, and later come to visit my grave, than the place he fondly remembers from his childhood as the place where he and I used to walk and eat cookies. I cannot.

This particular cemetery is owned by one of the large corporations, however, the people who work there are very much local and very service minded. That being said I encourage you to look at all funeral service providers, regardless of business ownership.

Though I touched on it briefly before, I want to reiterate that positive memory pictures are an important part of life and death. A perfect example of this is in Glendale, California, where Forest Lawn Cemetery has maintained and managed one of the most wonderful full life service centers and cemeteries that I have ever had the pleasure to walk the grounds of.

In fact, I used to have my office on Brand Avenue in Glendale. At that time, during my lunch breaks I would drive down Brand to the corner of Cerritos Street where Gold Star Hamburgers is located, just one block west of the Forest Lawn gates. I would pick up what has to be the world's greatest hamburger and drive up to the top of the hill at Forest Lawn and park across from the Freedom Mausoleum. There I had a view of the San Fernando Valley and Los Angeles Basin, and past Santa Monica all the way out to the bay. I would sit in my car with the windows down and enjoying the cool breeze. I would eat my lunch in the shade of a grove of old growth trees.

Forest Lawn truly is a wonderful place, and I love taking friends and family on tours of their artwork and buildings. The artwork coupled with the well kept grounds creates a very peaceful setting in the middle of chaotic Los Angeles.

Hubert Eaton founded Forest Lawn on New Year's Day 1917. He was truly a visionary man. He viewed Forest Lawn as a place full of life, not just another cemetery, but a place where children would be christened and blessed, where couples would marry, and loved ones would be laid to rest. As a matter of fact both Ronald Reagan and Regis Philbin, along with hundreds of others have had their weddings held at Forest Lawn.

Chapter Ten

Incredible ends of ordinary lives

What are the last words spoken by every "redneck" just before he dies? The answer: "Hey, watch this!" In this modern world of people being famous for being famous, reality show stars, YouTube celebrities, and TV shows based on America's next this or that, ordinary people are being propelled into the public eye, and at times it leads to a tragic end. Other times the tragic end of an ordinary person is so sensational that their manner or cause of death becomes known the world around.

I recall riding in the car with my mom, not more than a year ago, when the radio news announced that a man in Washington State had died as a result of injuries sustained while having sex with a horse. Not the most awkward car ride I've ever been on, but the news did create that awkward silence. My mom then asked, "Why would a guy die from having sex with a horse?" Completely understanding the thought process my mother was going through, I said, "The horse was having sex with him." I'll never forget the look of complete shock on my mother's face. Therefore, I will never forget the death of that man. However, knowing this is a litigious culture, I will omit the man's name from this book. I trust you know how to use an internet search engine.

However, there are times when in search of one's fifteen minutes of fame a person will lose their life. Take for example the tragic death of Scott Amedure, who is known to the world as the "Jenny Jones Murder".

Scott was a 32 year old bartender from Michigan. Unfortunately for Scott, he responded to Jenny Jones' request for those with secret crushes to revel them on her show. Scott's secret crush was for a man named Jonathan Schmitz. Jonathan worked for the Fox and the Hound restaurant in Bloomfield Hills, Michigan. Jonathan also had a number of unsuccessful suicide attempts and a history of manic behavior. Jonathan was also engaged to be married.

Unfortunately, for everyone involved, neither Jenny Jones nor the producers of her show ever did a psychological exam on this suicidal, manic person before booking him on the show.

Neither Jenny nor the producers even informed Jonathan that his "secret admirer" was a man with a homosexual crush on him prior to it being announced on national television.

While on TV Jonathan acted nicely and said that he was most definitely "heterosexual", he also played it off by saying that he was "flattered". However, when the pair returned to Michigan, they got together for drinks and appeared to be playing nice. However, Scott mistook these gestures as receptiveness to his advancements. Unfortunately he had misread Jonathan completely.

On the night of March 8, 1995, Scott left a blinking construction sign at Jonathan's door with a sign attached that read, "If you want to turn this off you will have to use your tool." The following morning Jonathan went to Gary's Guns, purchased a 12 gauge shotgun, and headed over to Scott's house.

Jonathan arrived at Scott's house just after 11a.m. and knocked on his door. After Scott answered, Jonathan asked him if he left the "thingy" at his door. After Scott confirmed his suspicions, Jonathan told him that he'd left something in his truck. Upon Jonathan's return, he promptly empties two rounds into Scott's chest. Oddly enough, Scott had tried to defend himself by holding out a wicker chair in front of him. Jonathan then called 9-1-1 to report what he had done.

Scott's death is a sad tribute to day-time talk shows that care only for ratings and not for the lives they harm or even end. Following Scotts death, his family was awarded $25 million dollars as a result of their wrongful death claim against Jenny Jones. Jonathan is now serving a 25-50 years sentence for murdering Scott.

For those in search of fame, there are few who have become greater symbols of failure and tragedy than Lillian M. Entwistle. Lillian was born in Port Talbot, Wales, in 1908. She spent her early years living in London. Her mom died young, and by the time she was fourteen, she had left for America to pursue an acting career. She was having some luck, by 1931; she had roles in eight consecutive Broadway shows. However, they all had failed to be successful.

Lillian with stars in her eyes and dreams of making it big thought that she would be more successful in Hollywood. Lillian and her Uncle Harold moved into a small home in Beachwood Canyon, with the famous HOLLYWOOD sign just at the end of her street and up the hill. In her day the sign originally read "Hollywoodland", and was an advertisement for a realty company.

She found work in Hollywood and played opposite Billie Burke in the play, "The Mad Hopes". She was also offered a contract with RKO Studios. Her first film was "The 13 Women", and her part was mostly edited out in post production.

Lillian then really wanted more work. She went on several auditions, and kept waiting for call backs. She had decided that she needed to earn enough money to travel back to New York. Sadly, she could not manage to save enough money for the train fare.

On Sunday, September 18, 1932, she told her Uncle Harold that she was going to visit some friends and would walk up Beachwood Drive to the drug store. That is not what she did. Instead, she walked to the large "H" of the landmark sign at the end of her street and used a maintenance ladder to climb to the top, and she then jumped to her death.

The next morning, an unknown female called the Los Angeles Police Department and said, "I was hiking near the Hollywoodland sign today and near the bottom I found a woman's shoe and jacket. A little further on I noticed a purse. In it was a suicide note. I looked down the mountain and saw a body. I don't want any publicity in this matter, so I wrapped up the jacket, shoes and purse in a bundle and laid them on the steps of the Hollywood Police Station." The woman then hung up.

The Los Angeles Times published the suicide note, in an effort to aid law enforcement in the identification of the unknown jumper. The note read: "I am afraid I am a coward. I am sorry for everything. P.E." Lillian's uncle, Harold, recognized the initials of her stage name and later identified her body at the morgue.

Lillian's funeral was held at the Strother's Mortuary, which at the time was located on Hollywood Boulevard, across the street from the Pantage's Theater. There is now a Metro Train Station there. After her funeral, her body was cremated at Hollywood Memorial Park and shipped to Ohio for burial, at Oak Hill Cemetery, Glendale, Ohio, where she was interred with her father on January 5, 1933.

While some have lost their life in search of fame, others have become famous just by having the pleasure of sharing their death experience with a celebrity. That was the case of Roger Arthur Peterson who at the age of twenty-one became a part of Rock-N-Roll history. Roger was the pilot of the aircraft whose crash took the lives of musicians Buddy Holly, Ritchie Valens and J.P. "The Big Bopper" Richardson as well as Roger's. The event came to be known as "The Day the Music Died".

Roger Peterson was born and raised in Alta, Iowa, the first of four children born to Arthur and Pearl Peterson. Roger had been employed as a pilot in Mason City, Iowa by Dwyer Flying Service. According to the Civil Aeronautics Board's Accident Report, by 1959, Peterson had been flying for over four years, receiving his private pilot's certificate in October 1954 and commercial pilot's certificate in April 1958.

Roger Peterson had married Deanne Lenz, whom he had been dating since high school, just months before he was killed. The couple resided in Clearlake, Iowa, only a few miles from Mason City where they both worked.

Just weeks prior to the crash, Roger earned his certification as a limited Flight Instructor, though he had not been granted his instrument rating, having only accumulated fifty-two hours as such and he also was not rated for night-time flying commercially. Peterson's total flying time was listed as 711 hours experience. He had spent 128 hours of those hours in the type of plane which claimed his life.

On the evening of February 2, 1959, the manager of the Surf Ballroom in Clearlake contacted Peterson to arrange a charter flight from Mason City to Fargo, North Dakota. The Surf was hosting the Winter Dance Party that evening and Buddy Holly, wanted to fly ahead of the rest of the tour members, who were traveling by bus. Peterson agreed to take the flight, and when the performers arrived at the airport, he learned that in addition to Holly, his other two passengers would be Ritchie Valens and J.P. "The Big Bopper" Richardson. Originally scheduled to fly with Holly that night were his guitar player, Tommy Allsup and his bass player, Waylon Jennings. Tommy gave his seat to Ritchie, via a coin toss, and Waylon gave his seat to J.P. since "The Bopper" had been sick.

The plane, a 1947 Beechcraft Bonanza (N3794N), departed in light snow from Mason City Airport around 1:00a.m. of February 3, 1959. The plane turned 180 degrees to the left and aimed north, achieving an altitude of 2,000 feet, cleared the airport, turned toward north-west and faded from view. Moments later the Beechcraft crashed in a cornfield five miles northwest of the airfield, killing all on board instantly.

The Civil Aeronautics Board concluded that the cause of the crash was pilot error due to Roger's inability to accurately interpret the Sperry F3 attitude indicator which he was forced to rely upon in poor weather conditions. The conventional theory is that Peterson read the unusual gyroscope, as if it was a conventional gyro. This would have lead him to believe that the plane was gaining altitude when it was actually descending. A secondary factor was that, although Roger called a number of times that evening for weather updates, he had not been informed of adverse flash weather forecasts.

A memorial service was held for Roger at Redeemer Lutheran Church, in Ventura, Iowa on February 5th. A funeral was held the next day at St. Paul Lutheran Church in his hometown of Alta; Roger was laid to rest in Buena Vista Memorial Cemetery in Storm Lake. Roger's parents would later receive condolence letters from the families of Holly and Valens.

In June 1988, in tribute to those killed that night, a 4-foot-tall granite monument bearing the names of all four passengers was dedicated outside the Surf Ballroom with Roger's widow, parents and sister in attendance; the event marked the first time that the families of Holly, Richardson, Valens, and Peterson had gathered together.

Chapter Eleven

Ordinary ends of incredible lives

There is a certain segment of the population that loves to grave hunt, and some people even visit the death scenes of famous individuals. Without reservation, I can say that there are only two resources that standout among the crowd for those who enjoy these activities. Both are websites, the first being WWW.FINDAGRAVE.COM and the second being WWW.FINDADEATH.COM .

The FINDAGRAVE.COM website is one of, if not the largest, publicly available registries of graves on the internet. Millions of grave locations, biographies, and often times they'll have photos of the deceased and their final resting place available to you all with the click of a button. I regularly check out this website when I travel. You can find local legends, funny headstones, historical figures, or any number of distant relatives.

A man named Scott Michaels is the mind behind my favorite death related website.

FINDADEATH.COM, by far is the most colorful, entertaining, and downright informative website when it comes to celebrity death. Scott puts significant time and effort into his research, and has successfully managed to operate the most accurate celebrity death chronicle that I have ever viewed.

Scott also operates "Dearly Departed Tours" in Hollywood, CA. For any individual traveling to Los Angeles, his tour is a must see event. I have been on a number of tours with visiting family members and friends; Scott's tours are always more fun, and much more informative than other "Star Tours". I say: Who cares where Billy Baldwin lives? Show me where River Phoenix died!

It is the love of celebrities; the mania surrounding their deaths (think Anna Nicole Smith and Michael Jackson) that makes Hollywood's history so much more entertaining than the movies it creates. While some celebrities steal the lime light even in death, there have been legendary icons that have slipped from this life into the next with little fanfare or craze.

Hollywood is full of characters; however, few will ever be able to match wit, talent, or prestige with Lucille Ball. Lucy was a very funny lady, and a brilliant business woman.

On Tuesday April 18, 1989 Lucy was at her home, located in Beverly Hills, when she started experiencing severe chest pains. Her husband, at that time, Gary Morton called the paramedics and they rushed her to the Emergency Room of Cedars-Sinai Medical Center where she underwent bypass surgery for nearly eight hours.

Lucy received the gift of life, via organ donation in the form of an aorta, from a 27-year-old male victim of a motorcycle crash. The following day, Lucy awakened and asked her husband, "How's the dog doing?" Her husband released a statement to the press that stated: "Her Irish eyes are smiling."

A few days thereafter, and described as "suddenly and without warning", her aorta burst. Doctors stated that the rupture occurred far from where a portion of her aortic valve was replaced during surgery. On Wednesday, April 26, 1989, at 6a.m., the world lost Lucy. She was 77 years old.

Lucy's funeral was private, however, there were three public memorial services scheduled around the country. One was held in Los Angeles, another in Chicago, and one in New York City. They were all held at 8p.m. on Monday, May 8th. The day and time was selected because it was the same time that the **I Love Lucy** television show used to air. Lucy was cremated, and she was interred in the Columbarium of Radiant Dawn, at Forest Lawn Cemetery, Hollywood Hills.

In March of 2002, Lucy's children had her remains moved from Forest Lawn, and reburied in Lucy's hometown of Jamestown, NY, where she is now a tourist attraction in a place in which her children have a financial interest.

While Lucy led the way for many female comics and studio executives, the color barrier was brought down in large part by the efforts and antics of one of the most entertaining men the world has ever known. Sammy Davis Jr. is quoted as saying, "Being a star made it possible for me to get insulted in places where the average Negro could never hope to go and get insulted."

Sadly, many of us are not old enough to remember the vibe and the spectacle that was the "Rat Pack". Frank Sinatra, Dean Martin, Peter Lawford, Joey Bishop and Sammy Davis Jr. entertained million, made millions and became the poster boys for everything cool.

In September of 1989, Sammy was diagnosed with throat cancer and went through radiation treatment. Sammy's last live performance was at Harrah's in Lake Tahoe, just hours before his first radiation treatment. Everyone had thought that the cancer was under control, that was, until the following February.

When it was obvious that Sammy would not be around much longer, a television special was planned, it was a two and a half-hour tribute to Sammy, which he attended. At the conclusion of the show Sammy got up, unable to speak; he did a little soft-shoe, and received a standing ovation.

Weeks later, Sammy's health deteriorated and he was admitted to Cedars Sinai. On March 13th, Sammy was released, and went home to die. One report stated that he had dwindled down to only sixty pounds. According to the National Enquirer, Frank Sinatra visited him and "A softball size tumor stuck out of Sammy's neck, giving off a horrible odor. And the sight devastated Sinatra."

Sammy died on Wednesday, May 16th, (the same day as Muppets creator Jim Henson) at his home in Beverly Hills. He was 64 years old. By the time they removed Sammy's body from his home, hundreds of people lined the streets. That night, the lights on the Las Vegas Strip were dimmed for 10 minutes.

Sammy's funeral was open to the public, and on Friday morning, 400 tickets were given to those that got to Forest Lawn early enough. People had started lining up at 6a.m.. It was an open casket service. Over 1,200 people packed the church, and hundreds more were mourning outside. "I've Got To Be Me" was played on the loudspeaker, and the crowd cheered. The service lasted for ninety minutes. The Reverend Jesse Jackson eulogized him. Frank Sinatra, Dean Martin, Michael Jackson and Bill Cosby were honorary pallbearers. Although Sammy's funeral was held at Forest Lawn Hollywood Hills, he was buried at Forest Lawn Glendale. Oddly enough, this is the same scenario that played out years later for Michael Jackson's funeral and burial.

While Hollywood has created countless celebrities, it had only a small supporting role for the man who is the one 20th Century icon that stands above all others for crossing over from athlete to page-one celebrity: Joe DiMaggio.

In a time before a 24-hour TV news cycle, ESPN, or even the internet littered with websites devoted to celebrity Joe DiMaggio, went from the sports page to the tabloids. The major reasons why: He was a Hall of Fame baseball player who holds records that will never be broken; his short, and stormy marriage to Marilyn Monroe; and the legend that grew from the 1968 Simon and Garfunkel song "Mrs. Robinson".

DiMaggio's death occurred March 8, 1999, in his Hollywood, Florida, home. His death was anticipated by newspaper writers and television news producers. DiMaggio tribute packages were prerecorded or ready to roll off the presses; mainly because he had been on death's doorstep for at least six months. During that time, he had received last rites and had slipped in and out of a coma a number of times.

During his life he kept to himself and was intensely private. Teammates who played with him for 10 years never had dinner with him. When rookie Mickey Mantle joined the team in 1950, DiMaggio frightened him so much that Mick never spoke to him during his entire first season. "He's one of the loneliest guys I ever knew," teammate Eddie Lopat once said, "and he leads the league in room service."

His economically poor roots were immortalized in Ernest Hemingway's "The Old Man and the Sea". I would like to take the great DiMaggio fishing," the Hemingway character

Santiago says. "…maybe he was as poor as we are and would understand."

In 1951, DiMaggio was recently retired and didn't know what to do with himself. He was introduced to Marilyn Monroe at the midtown Manhattan saloon Toots Shor's, located at 51 West 51st Street. This had become one of Joe's favorite places to hang out. They dated for about a year, before they married in San Francisco, at City Hall. He was 40, and she was 28 years old. Monroe's career was taking off like a rocket, while the private DiMaggio hid from the limelight. Marriage to the curvy bombshell created a media firestorm.

The marriage was a rocky one from the beginning. After marrying and spending their honeymoon night in a $6.50 motel room, they flew to Japan, where Monroe was scheduled to entertain the U.S. troops in South Korea. As the famous story goes, upon her return to the hotel, Monroe gushed, "Joe, you never heard such cheering!" "Yes, I have," DiMaggio said quietly, but not without a hint of mocking at his clueless wife. Could it be possible that she forgot his nine World Series rings? The news of their divorce after 274 days was hardly a shock.

DiMaggio never remarried. After Marilyn's death on August 5, 1962, he made sure fresh roses were always at her grave at Westwood Memorial Park. Rumor has it that the couple was attempting reconciliation before her mysterious death. He was repeatedly offered huge sums to write a book about their marriage, but he never granted a single interview about Marilyn. About the only quote he ever gave was to boxing writer Bert Sugar, who had the nerve to ask what it was like to be with Monroe. "Better than rooming with Joe Page," was his reply.

Joe DiMaggio's last appearance in public September 27, 1998, when he was honored at the "Joe DiMaggio Day", and was presented with replicas of his nine World Series rings, which had been stolen from a hotel room decades earlier.

Unfortunately, death for DiMaggio was long and painful. For six months straight, his health woes were in the news daily. On October 12, 1998, his lawyer Morris Engelberg said Joe was checking into Regional Memorial Hospital in Hollywood, FL, because of pneumonia. DiMaggio was unaware that he had cancer.

Joe had lung cancer, and the doctors operated. During his ninety-nine days in the hospital, DiMaggio suffered a series of health setbacks. Each time, news reports came out that he was near death. Including an incident that occurred during the NCAA Final Four Basketball Tournament, in which CBS reported that he was dead. In fact, DiMaggio was watching the game.

After a cancerous tumor was removed from DiMaggio's right lung on October 14, 1998, he required two bronchoscope procedures to drain excess fluid from the lung. Just a month later, on November 16th, his blood pressure dropped and his family summoned a priest to perform "Last Rites". To the world, it was only said that DiMaggio had been "very ill" and it wasn't until November 24th that his lung cancer was publicly revealed. The following day was his 84th birthday.

Joe battled multiple infections and cancer. A breathing tube had been inserted into his throat during the course of his treatment. Upon removal of the tube Joe was able to speak for the first time on December 3rd. "I want to get the hell out of here and go home!" was his plea.

On December 4th, a fever accompanied by lung congestion flared again, and this was compounded by an intestinal infection. On December 11th, DiMaggio was in a coma for 18 hours. To his doctors' amazement, he pulled through. He was released from the hospital on January 19, 1999, to his home in Hollywood, Florida. He died there on Monday, March 8th, surrounded by family and a few friends. He was 84 years old. A private plane flew his body back to San Francisco.

Father Armand Oliveri, who grew up with DiMaggio, celebrated the Mass of Christian burial. DiMaggio's younger brother, former Red Sox all-star Dominic "Dom" DiMaggio, delivered the eulogy. Dominic spoke about his brother's desire for privacy, his love of children, and the one big thing missing from his life: love of a woman.

Dom DiMaggio said that his twice-divorced brother had everything in his record-setting baseball career, except for the right woman to share his life. To fill that void, Dom said, that his brother dedicated his life away from baseball to helping children, including establishing a children's wing in a hospital in Hollywood, Florida.

Pallbearers were Joe's son, Joe DiMaggio Jr. (who died a few months after the funeral of his father of an apparent heart attack), Roger Stein and James Hamra, the husbands of DiMaggio's two granddaughters; Joseph DiMaggio, son of the player's late brother, Mike; Joe Nacchio, a friend of

DiMaggio's for 59 years; and his lawyer, Morris Engelberg. DiMaggio's graveside service, like his funeral Mass, was attended by about 50 family members and close friends. DiMaggio had requested the invitation-only services. No Yankees, past or present, were invited.

San Francisco Police cordoned off about 300 fans and reporters in a park across the street from Saints Peter and Paul Church; located in San Francisco's Italian enclave of North Beach, where DiMaggio had spent his childhood. The gathered crowd burst into spontaneous applause and shouted "bravo" as the brown casket covered with white flowers was carried down the steps of the church at the conclusion of the service.

DiMaggio was temporarily entombed March 11, 1999, in a family mausoleum at Holy Cross Cemetery located in Colma, California. The San Francisco Catholic Diocese said that a permanent mausoleum for DiMaggio would be built later.

The most fitting tribute to Joe DiMaggio was held at Yankee Stadium in April of 1999. The Yankees unveiled a stone monument in the outfield memorial garden, where tributes to greats such as Lou Gehrig, Babe Ruth and Mickey Mantle have been erected. Before the first pitch, the outfield wall opened up, and Paul Simon strode to the spot where "Joltin' Joe" used to patrol; and he performed "Mrs. Robinson".

Fewer people have had an impact on entrainment and Americana as Walter "Walt" Elias Disney; books and volumes have been filled detailing his contributions to the art of animation, theme park design, and the motion picture industry. He won twenty-nine Academy Awards and was nominated a total of fifty-nine times.

On November 22, 1966, Walt was diagnosed with lung cancer, caused by many years of smoking. His preferred brand was unfiltered Lucky Strikes, but later switched to Gitanes, French cigarettes.

The cancer was discovered while undergoing pre-op screening for neck surgery to repair a nagging polo injury at St. Joseph Hospital in Burbank, CA. An X-ray revealed a tumor. The actual quote is, "his left lung was riddled with tumors the size of walnuts." Immediate surgery on his left lung was advised. However, Walt checked out to attend to studio business and then re-entered the hospital later. Surgery was performed the next day and his left lung was found to be cancerous and was removed.

After two weeks of post surgery rehabilitation, he was released from the hospital. After spending Thanksgiving Day with his family, he collapsed at his home located in Palm Springs. On November 30th, he was driven back to St. Joseph's Hospital in Burbank. He lost consciousness regularly in the days to come. Walt spent his 65th birthday in the hospital with his wife and children at his bedside.

His wife Lillian spent some time with him on December 14th, and he was visited by his brother Roy in the evening; Roy left the room crying. Roy ordered the lights at the Disney Studio, located across the street, to stay on at all times while Walt was in the hospital. Walt would ask the nurses to prop him up so he could see the studios. He died a few hours later, at 9:30a.m. on Thursday, December 15, 1966.

Disney's funeral was held at the Little Church of the Flowers at Forest Lawn Cemetery in Glendale, at 5:00p.m. on December 16th. No announcements of his funeral were made and only close relatives were in attendance. Walt did not like funerals and rarely attended one. During his life, he made it clear that he wished not to have a funeral. His daughter Diane once quoted her father as saying, "When I'm dead I don't want a funeral. I want people to remember me alive."

Walt Disney was cremated and his cremated remains were interred in a vault at Forest Lawn Cemetery, Glendale, in a semi-private garden, located just to the left of the entrance to the Freedom Mausoleum. A rumor spread after Walt's death that he was cryogenically frozen, but his family has always denied this and all known evidence refutes these rumors.

There are few who can say that they were once a Beatle. George Harrison was one of them, and a musical visionary, and also a very private person. George was also a heavy smoker, and developed lung cancer after having fought a battle against throat cancer. On November 7, 2001, George was supposedly receiving cancer treatment in Staten Island University Hospital under the name Arias, the maiden name of his wife. Apparently during his hospital stay, he got in touch with security man Gavin de Becker. De Becker does a lot of celebrity security, and they began to map out plans for a secretive funeral for George. George decided he would not return to his mansion in the UK, and he refused to die in a hospital. It is believed that this is when Paul McCartney stepped up and offered his own home in Beverly Hills.

George left the hospital and headed to Los Angeles, with assistance from the doctors of the UCLA Medical Center, with pain management medication. He then settled in at Paul's house on Heather Street in Beverly Hills, to die. It was approximately thirty-six hours of George drifting in and out of consciousness, with his wife and son at his side. One of the non-family members allowed was George's friend Ravi Shankar, who played sitar music.

According to Shankar, George placed pictures of the Hindu gods Krishna and Rama around his bed, and he chanted the Krishna mantra. Additionally, two of George's close friends from the Krishna faith, Shayam Sundara and Mukunda, were there also chanting quietly into their meditation beads, while George passed away at 1:20p.m. on November 29, 2001. He was 58 years old.

His body was then wrapped in a shawl, and covered with holy oils. Approximately twenty minutes after his death, first call personnel from Hollywood Forever Cemetery arrived to remove George's remains. They briefly joined hands with the Harrison family and the security staff, and said a small prayer. As they made their way to the funeral home, they made a brief stop at the doctor's office in their unmarked white van. The doctor signed George's death certificate. George was cremated in a cardboard "alternative container", within 10 hours of his death. George was cremated in the same crematory that Mama Cass was cremated in decades earlier.

George's cremated remains were released to his family, and they took him to their home in Hawaii, and then on to India where he was scattered in the Ganges River, in accordance with the Krishna faith.

The staff at the funeral home, most likely at the family's request, put a phony address as the place of death on George's death certificate. Gloria Allred, who has never met a microphone that she didn't like, made it her job to make sure the "correct" information was registered with the county. The County of Los Angeles released an updated death certificate with de Becker's address on it. George's family even released a photo of George and Olivia standing in front of de Becker's mailbox. However, the facts and statements from those who were at George's death scene indicate that, George really did die in Paul McCartney's home. It is widely accepted that George's family is attempting to keep the exact location of George's death a mystery in an effort to prevent the location from becoming a shrine for Beatles fans to gather.

Very few people are considered to be more American than Bob Hope. However, Bob Hope was born Leslie Townes Hope in England on May 29, 1903. His family later immigrated to America, when he was four years old, settling in Cleveland, Ohio.

Bob stopped doing television specials in 1996, and all but retired from show business. In May of 1998, on his 95th birthday, he and his wife Dolores celebrated with a party that was held at their Toluca Lake house, which they had lived in since 1938.

Three days later, on May 30th, he and Dolores were the honorary grand marshals for a Toluca Lake parade that was held in his honor. Days later in June of 1998, it was reported that Bob had died. This was not the case, his daughter Linda made the statement; "He was eating breakfast when he heard about it. He got a big laugh out of it".

From that point on, Bob's health steadily deteriorated. He was in and out of the hospital, in June of 2000, he was hospitalized for severe gastrointestinal bleeding. The next year, in August of 2001, he was hospitalized again with pneumonia.

Sadly as a result of the many eye operations that had been performed on him over the years, his eyes were unable to form tears, and they were constantly red. Additionally, Bob was almost completely blind and had great difficulty walking.

Bob celebrated his 100th birthday with family and friends. His granddaughter Miranda is quoted as saying, "Despite his deteriorating health, he still expressed his good sense of humor, and was able to say he was still with us".

On Sunday, July 27, 2003, Bob died of pneumonia, with family present. Bob's daughter Linda said that, "Dad had an amazing send-off. All of the family was together with him and he died very peacefully last night, just about 9:30p.m.. I don't think you could have asked for a more peaceful, beautiful death. And I think all the good vibes that he put out during his lifetime came back to take him up. He left us with a smile on his face and no last words. We all had our little time with him and time to say good-bye. And he just gave us each a kiss, and that was it."

The following day, President George W. Bush paid tribute to Bob by saying, "Bob Hope made us laugh, and he lifted our spirits. Bob Hope served our nation. He went to battlefields to entertain thousands of troops from different generations. We extend our prayers to his family, and we will mourn the loss of a good man. May God bless his soul."

Approximately 900 people attended a memorial service for Bob on August 27th, at the St. Charles Borromeo Roman Catholic Church in North Hollywood. Some of the more notable attendees included Phyllis Diller, Barbara Eden, Marie Osmond, Gerald Ford, Nancy Reagan, Brooke Shields, Larry King, Kelsey Grammer and Loni Anderson.

Bob Hope was buried on August 28th, in the San Fernando Mission Cemetery, in Mission Hills, Los Angeles. Bob's grave is located in a gated courtyard within the mission's walls, and to pay your respects, you are also asked to pay an admission fee.

Chapter 12

The days we wish we were somebody else

I have known people from nearly every professional walk of life, and I've come to learn that there is no perfect job, or any amount of money to compensate for certain aspects of any given profession; and certainly that every job comes with sacrifices and tradeoffs. This is especially true in the mortuary business.

Within the walls of the funeral home employees see, hear, touch and smell things that make us, as morticians, wish that we would have followed the path into another profession. Such occurrences happen so frequently that one can scarcely begin to enumerate their total over the lifetime of any individual's career.

This chapter recounts and illustrates some of the odd, unusual and disturbing things experienced by the average mortician. If you believe that you may be sensitive to reading such accounts, please spare yourself the burden. I promise that I won't be offended.

Countless times I have been asked the question: "What's the grossest thing you have ever seen?" The answer: "That all depends on what you think is gross."

Furthermore, I think it to be rather odd that one would ask such a question. I think that asking such a question would be a kin to asking an individual how many people they killed during the war. I would caution you against asking any individual what was the most psychologically damaging thing they have ever witnessed.

What I saw as a mortician, never really bothered me, or so I thought at the time. Sights were really the least of my worries. However, I now know that what I saw has seared its way into my memories, and the visual cues that I see on a daily basis are viewed thru a rather warped lens.

Berry cobbler, for instance, when viewed from the side strangely resembles the fat and tissue layers of the human abdomen as seen after the "Y" incision has been made during the course of an autopsy. One might think that this type of visual memory would dissuade me from eating cobblers, it does not. If I stopped eating everything that held a memory of death or resemblance to something that I viewed in the preparation room of the funeral home, I scarcely would eat again. I certainly would never enjoy another barbecue, and I am just not willing to give that up.

Likewise, seeing the sight of injuries to another person is just not as alarming to me as they may be to others. I have seen friends and family members with dislocated bones, compound fractures, third degree burns and other substantially serious injuries; only to view them as a minor setback, not as sights of horror. I even viewed professional hockey player Clint Malarchuk's on ice throat cutting as a "Wow, that could have been bad," moment, and not as a "that's terrible" instant in time.

As an embalmer I had to repair the damaged body of a young man whose parachute failed to open. What a mess that was. Truly, aside from being a mass of battered and broken bones all that was really recognizable was his hands. However, the damage to his body was not nearly as heart wrenching to me as the utter look of devastation in his mother's eye. Mortuary college taught me how to recreate a head that had gone missing, or been destroyed; however, few things can prepare an individual for the sight of despair witnessed as a parent views their dead child.

We, as modern Americans, are a very visual culture. Few oppose, or believe in, what they cannot see. That is why photo journalism is such an important form of media today. How many of us would care about those in Sudan or Tibet, if not for the photographic evidence of their plight? Simple images can create a lasting bond between two people who have never met.

However, one of the major issues facing the mortuary business and their relationship with the consumer is that no one really knows what their getting for their money. Nobody sees what goes on behind the closed doors of the funeral home. This is unfortunate for all involved. I believe that if the families were more intimately involved with the disposition of their loved ones, they would have a greater respect for their local mortician. Several cultures help dress, shroud or otherwise prepare their deceased loved ones; and seldom have I heard a complaint about pricing from these sects of society. They actually seem to have a genuine fondness and reverence for their mortician.

While sights are unforgettable, I have learned that smells never really vanish. For example, every time I smell a juniper I think of my grandma's house. It is a smell that I will never forget. Unfortunately, I wish I could forget a number of the smells that I encountered while working in the mortuary business. Having had the opportunity to not only work in a funeral home, but also in a crematory and cemetery; my nose has been the entry point of many foul memories.

In the course of writing this book, fewer tasks have been more challenging than trying to describe an odor that most have not smelled. I can only compare it to describing the color red to one who is blind? Oddly enough, I am describing odors to you that I hope you never smell.

We have all had similar life experiences with unpleasant odors; such as walking into the bathroom after your father on chili night; or the smell of the dirty diaper that has been in the trashcan too long; or the dumpster that really needs to be pressure washed, or the smell of that dead dog or cat that didn't answer when called. However, there are a handful of odors that a mortician will smell and immediately be frustrated with having to find a solution for.

The term "Tissue Gas" strikes fear in the heart of every embalmer. Tissue gas is the name given to the action of the bacteria Clostridium Perfringens (formerly known as *C. Welchii*) in dead bodies. Its effect on the deceased is that of extremely accelerated decomposition. Tissue gas is only halted or slowed by embalming the body and during the embalming process special additive chemicals must be employed. Tissue gas most commonly occurs in the bodies of people who have died of gangrene, large decubitus ulcers, necrotizing fasciitis or who have had soil or water forced into wounds.

Tissue gas and the resulting odor is the most unique stench encountered in the mortuary business. The smell of tissue gas is very similar to advanced decomposition, but sweeter. It is an oddly "light" odor that is unmistakably dissimilar to any other.

Another unmistakable odor is that of lung cancer. A number of years ago I saw a report on the television news about dogs that were being successfully trained to "sniff out" cancer in an effort to achieve earlier diagnosis. I believe this is possible. Cancer is a horrible smelling decease. If a dog can be trained to smell drugs through a suitcase, then I am certain they can be trained to smell cancer in the human body.

I first smelled lung cancer when I was seventeen years old. It was in an old Victorian house that had small rooms and narrow hallways.

The deceased was an elderly woman, and very slender, that had died in the back bedroom of the house. The room was only accessible by walking down an "L" shaped hallway. This prevented us from being able to get our gurney completely down the hall and into the room where she laid in bed. Her being of slight build made it easier to carry her in our arms, however, the halls were very narrow and we were required to hold her very close in such tight quarters. In a move that I can only describe as being similar to a weight lifters "curl" I lifted the body of the deceased into my chest. By doing this, I caused in the deceased what can only be described as a postmortem "exhaling". The decease expelled my never to be forgotten first exposure to the stench of cancer.

Another smell that I learned to dread was found at funeral services. The smell would make your eyes water. I could barely stand the exposure to it. A church filled with ladies and gentlemen all wearing unique perfumes. Oh what a horrible odor. It can only be described as a cacophony of nasal noise. That pungent rose smelling perfume was the greatest offender. Match that with an assortment of

Old Spice, Brut, Stetson, and countless other perfumes and your nose will beg for mercy. A stuffy church on a hot July day with a large crowd, and you will be searching for fresh air.

While I have seen and smelled things that I can't clear from my mind, it took me a while to fully appreciate how sounds can haunt your memory.

The first "sound" that I learned to both recognize and fear within the funeral business was the sound of "purge" as it made its way from the stomach to the mouth. Anyone who has ever siphoned gasoline or used a similar method to empty a fish tank will recall the noise the fluid made as it traveled the length of the hose. A plumber might be able to describe the noise they hear as they clear a pipe and fluid travels the length on its way to the sewer system. Nothing will remind you more urgently that you have allowed the stomach of the deceased to get higher than the head than the sound of purge making its way out of the body.

Late in my funeral service career I came across a sound that I could have never imagined existed. It is the only time that I ever heard something that made me nearly vomit.

It was the middle of the summer, and I had been called out to a trailer park. I may as well tell you now, as a mortician, nothing will ever go well for you in a trailer park. The cops were dispatched after a neighbor called in reporting a "foul" odor coming from the trailer; the neighbor was correct. There most certainly was a foul odor coming from that trailer. The deceased person, we couldn't even determine sex at the time, was sitting in a recliner with no air conditioning on for at least a couple of days. Advanced decomposition had set in, the body had bloated, and we quickly learned that the shirt he was wearing really wasn't a shirt at all - it was several layers of skin. This individual was a mess.

Bound by duty, and my employment agreement that paid me $65 per body that I removed, I moved in to remove this unfortunate individual's earthly remains. There were two of us there, and I stepped up to maneuver the upper body while my co-worker stepped up to manage the feet.

With a strong desire to get out of there in a hurry, we decided that one fast and smooth action would be our best plan of action. Even the best laid plans go wrong. As we quickly picked up the remains, we quickly became aware of the large "blister" that had formed on the un-clothed upper body of the deceased. As we lifted the body from the chair the "blister" broke emptying its contents onto the floor and chair. It sounded as if someone had dumped out the liquid contents of a five gallon bucket all at once. The stench coupled with that sound was just about as close as I ever came to losing my lunch on the job.

The next sound that I cannot forget is best summed up as opening a Velcro wallet. Some people live alone, and sadly, some people die alone. For those who die alone on a carpeted floor, and remain there for several days or weeks, when they are removed from the carpet the sound of a Velcro wallet opening is the best way to describe the sound of that process.

This chapter is not a comprehensive list of disturbing sights, foul odors, and disgusting sounds that a mortician will come across. From the sights of farming accidents, fire victims, and chemical burns, to the smells that accompany them, death knows no limits. Unfortunately, the mortician is the one who has to live with the damage left behind by death.